IN DISGUISE!

stories of real women spies

To the women who have worked, and will continue to work,
unknown and unsung, for freedom.
—PDG and EGM

Published by
Beyond Words Publishing, Inc.
20827 NW Cornell Road, Suite 500
Hillsboro, Oregon 97124
503-531-8700

Every effort has been made to contact the copyright owners of the photographs in this book. If the copyright holder of a photograph in this book has not heard from us, please contact Beyond Words Publishing. The publisher gratefully acknowledges and thanks the following for their generous assistance and permission to use photos:

Belle Boyd: Courtesy of Berkeley County Historical Society, WV
Gertrude S. Legendre: Courtesy of Medway Institute, SC
Maria Gulovich Liu: Courtesy of Maria Gulovich Liu
Marguerite Harrison: Courtesy of the Society of Woman Geographers, Washington, D.C.
Leona Vicario Roo: Courtesy of the Latin American Library, Tulane University
Josefa Ortiz de Dominguez: Courtesy of the Latin American Library, Tulane University
Elizabeth Van Lew: Courtesy of the Library of Virginia
Virginia Hall: Courtesy of Lorna Catling
Sarah Emma Edmonds: Courtesy of State Archives of Michigan

Special Thanks To: Robert Barnett, Jane Bedell, Kristin Hilton, Brenda Smith, and Kayt Zundel.

Library of Congress Cataloging-in-Publication Data

Hunter, Ryan Ann.
  In disguise! : stories of real women spies / written by Ryan Ann Hunter.
      p. cm.
Summary: A collection of biographies of real women who were spies throughout history and around the world, including Virginia Hall, Sarah Emma Edmonds, Josephine Baker, and Eva Wu.
  ISBN 1-58270-095-8
  1. Women spies—Biography—Juvenile literature. [1. Spies. 2. Women—Biography.] I. Title.

  UB270.5.H86 2003
  327.12'092'2—dc21   20030443

Printed in the United States of America
Distributed to the book trade by Publishers Group West

The corporate mission of Beyond Words Publishing, Inc.: *Inspire to Integrity*

IN DISGUISE!

stories of real women spies

written by **RYAN ANN HUNTER**

BEYOND
WORDS
Publishing
I N C

Ryan Ann Hunter is the pen name for Elizabeth G. Macalaster and Pamela D. Greenwood who write together.

Author Note

We chose the spies in this book for their daring deeds. Some of their stories were not recorded until long after they had happened. We've tried to study all accounts of their lives to make sure what we've included is true, but because these spies worked in secret, all the details about some of their activities will never be known. To make their stories come alive, we've filled in certain scenes with what could have happened in that time and place, being careful to respect the spies and their work.

Acknowledgements

The authors wish to thank the many people who helped with biographical research and in locating photos and images.

Pamela would like to thank: Joan Blacker, Everett Public Library, Everett, WA; Connie Sobel, Emma S. Clark Memorial Library, Setauket, NY; Greg Johnson, David Library of the American Revolution, Washington Crossing, PA; EZ Langston, a descendant of "Daring Dicey". Special thanks to Harriet Imrey who provided background on the American Revolutionary War battles and family histories in South Carolina.

Elizabeth would like to thank: Don Wood, Berkeley County Historical Society, Martinsburg, WV; Doris Walters, Medway Institute, Goose Creek, SC; Laird Easton, California State University at Chico, CA; John Baldwin, pilot; Lorna Catling, Virginia Hall's niece. A very special thanks to Maria Gulovich Liu and Jonna Mendez, who took time to share their experiences, review their profiles, and offer inspiration.

CONTENTS

INTRODUCTION

From the time people started spying—and that's probably been just about forever—women were part of it. And they were good!

Women dashed through enemy lines, sent secret messages under the nose of the enemy, and led prisoners in daring and dangerous escapes. They went undercover, taking new identities varying from apple sellers to crazy neighbors to beautiful stage dancers. Often, it was enough of a disguise for women to just be themselves. People didn't expect them to have the strength or know-how to be spies.

The spies in this book took their jobs for many reasons—excitement, foreign travel, a career, or a chance to fight for their beliefs. Some were involved in just one mission; others spied for years. Whatever their motives, they weren't content to sit back and let things happen. They were courageous. They were resourceful. They did what they had to do.

Few fit the mold of a typical woman or girl of their time. Some, like Emily Geiger, Belle Boyd, and Policarpa Salavarrieta, were in their teens when they began spying. Young as they were, they weren't afraid to risk their lives for their beliefs.

Television shows, movies, and books often portray spying as a glamorous profession. You might know a secret agent you'd like to be! Think twice. Along with the thrills, there's real danger. Spies can be caught, imprisoned, and even executed.

Being a secret agent isn't for everyone, but standing up for what you believe is something you can do. We hope the stories in this book will inspire you to be daring and brave and find courage when you need it. One person can make a difference!

The Anglo-Dutch Wars

In the seventeenth century, the Netherlands was a peaceful trading nation with one of the biggest merchant fleets in the world. The Dutch depended on their strong Navy and sea trade to keep their economy stable. They sailed to their colonies in Asia, Africa, the Caribbean, and South America, where they traded for spices, colorful cloth, and exotic plants. The Netherlands became a wealthy empire.

England, also a great maritime nation, wanted these trading routes. The Dutch didn't want to share. War was inevitable.

Three Anglo-Dutch wars were fought. At the end of the wars, the Dutch were defeated, and England gained control of the sea trade. During the second war, Charles II was King of England. While the Dutch had a good intelligence network, England's intelligence service had become sloppy and ineffective. England desperately needed reliable agents, even if it meant recruiting women as well as men.

APHRA BEHN

Ahead of Her Time

1640 – 1689

must warn the King, Aphra thought after her meeting with William Scot, another spy. Using the cipher code she had learned before leaving on her secret mission, Aphra sent her urgent warning to Lord Arlington:

Beware! The Dutch are planning to sail to England and up the Thames River to sink English ships. You must stop them!
— Agent 169

* * * *

Aphra Johnson was born in 1640 in the small town of Wye, near Canterbury, England. She was believed to be the daughter of a barber. As a young girl in the 1600s, Aphra had to follow strict rules. Dancing, card playing, and bright clothing were all banned. Girls knew their place. They were to be silent, obedient, and pious. But Aphra wasn't just any girl. She was bright, willful, and independent—a girl way ahead of her time.

While other girls embroidered and learned to cook, Aphra devoured books. She was hooked on French romances, which were full of emotion, heroism, and daring. Whenever she could, Aphra also read books about history, philosophy, and literature—anything that took her beyond her confining life.

Aphra liked to write, and she made up funny poems. She didn't have a lot of money to buy books, so she copied poems and plays. Many girls spent a lot of time on this activity, making pen quills from the feathers of geese and ravens. They drew lines, practiced their letters, and then erased the lines with bread.

At that time, girls received a different education from boys that included some reading, writing, a little math, and music. Aphra also was exposed to foreign languages from the many immigrants who had their hair cut at her father's shop as they passed through.

Early in 1663 Aphra's father was appointed governor of Surinam, a new English colony on the coast of South America. That fall, Aphra, her mother, father, sister, and younger brother set sail for the colony. What an adventure it would be! But on the way, Aphra's father was killed in a hurricane. Aphra and the rest of her family continued to the colony and lived there for six months. There she met William Scot, a political exile. He had been a spy in the English intelligence service, but he had gotten in trouble with the government and had been banished to Surinam.

The following spring, Aphra returned to England. She was already twenty-four years old—nearly too old to get married. (Most girls were married by the age of twenty). If you were unmarried at twenty-five, you were considered a lost cause, a spinster. Aphra had no inheritance, no dowry, and no income. Her only options other than marrying were to become a lady-in-waiting, a chamber maid, or someone's mistress.

Aphra didn't like any of these choices. She wanted to support herself by writing, but this was unthinkable for a lady of that time. Only men earned a living by writing plays and stories. So she married Mr. Behn, a London merchant, originally from Holland. (Not much is known about Mr. Behn, not even his first name.)

The marriage soon ended with Mr. Behn's death. The Great Plague ravaged London for more than a year. Merchants were especially vulnerable to this horrible disease, because they couldn't leave their businesses in London. Those who stayed in the city died by the thousands.

Mr. Behn didn't leave Aphra much money, and again she found herself in a desperate situation. Then an interesting opportunity presented itself. The king wanted Aphra to tell him all about Surinam. She told him how important the colony was and gave him dried butterflies, snake skins, and bright feathers from Surinam. Aphra was outgoing, funny, and good at mimicking people. The king liked her and invited her to spend more time at his court. With her pile of chestnut hair and decked out in ribbons and pearls, Aphra became very popular.

England and Holland were rivals in trade and had been at war on and off for several years. England had been worried for some time about a Dutch invasion. They needed a reliable spy in Holland. The king's intelligence office thought of Aphra. She was tall, attractive, enjoyed socializing, and knew Dutch. She would make the perfect undercover agent!

William Scot was already in Holland. English intelligence wanted Aphra to persuade William to spy again and reveal any Dutch plots against England. If William agreed, he'd be well paid and pardoned for his earlier mistakes.

How could Aphra turn down such an opportunity? How many other ladies had a job like this? Armed with instructions on how to send coded messages using a cipher, Secret Agent 169 sailed to Holland. She wasted no time in contacting William Scot, who gave her information about the Dutch fleet's plans to attack England.

But despite a steady stream of detailed letters to the head of English intelligence, he was indifferent to her. He didn't take her messages seriously, nor did he pay Aphra for her spying. She had to borrow money just to buy food and supplies. Still, Aphra regarded her mission as honorable and patriotic and continued sending dispatches—including the warning of the impending Dutch invasion.

Finally, Aphra got a loan from a friend, and in May 1667, she sailed back to England. She expected to be received at court with praise and back pay. She got neither.

And what of her warning? The king had refused to move on Aphra's intelligence. He believed that the Dutch would never dare invade England. But they did. Not a month after Aphra returned, the Dutch sailed up the Thames River. They set fire to many English ships moored in the river and captured the *Royal Charles*, the pride of the English navy. The English were stunned and humiliated.

Aphra tried unsuccessfully to get the king to pay her for her spying services. Finally, she was thrown in prison for not paying back the loans from her friends. Somehow, she was eventually released; perhaps relatives, friends, or even the king himself, finally paid her debt.

Nearly thirty, Aphra was now an ex-spy out of debtor's prison and a widow with no prospect of earning a living. Aphra needed to do something, but she wasn't about to try spying again.

Despite the impossible odds, Aphra Behn became a writer and the first English woman to live by writing. By the end of her life, Aphra had completed more than fifteen novels, seventeen plays, poetry, and translations from French and Latin. In her writing, Aphra created strong, independent, female characters who made their own choices, just as she had.

Aphra died at the age of forty-nine, pen in hand.

Spy
TRIVIA

The Trojan Horse, a seemingly innocent gift from the Greeks to the people of Troy, was really a clever disguise. Inside the horse were Greek soldiers ready to attack.

SPY SECRETS:
The Cardano Grille

Invented by Girolamo Cardano (1501 – 1576), the Cardano Grille was used to send secret messages. Back then, spies made the grille from wood, but you can just use cardboard.

You'll need:
> pencil or pen
> paper
> two pieces of cardboard the same size as the paper
> scissors

Follow these steps:
1. Think of a simple message you'd like to send a friend, like "Meet me tomorrow at the mall later."
2. Cut out word-sized squares or rectangles from different places in each piece of the cardboard. This is your grille. The number of cut-outs needs to match the number of words in your message.
3. Place the grille over the paper and write the words in your message in the cut-outs.
4. Remove the grille and fill in around your secret message with other words to form a note, part of homework assignment, etc.
5. Give your friend the note without the grille. Can she read the secret message?
6. No? Now give her the grille to decode your message.

* Steps 2,3, and 4 are illustrated on page 14.

The Cardano Grille

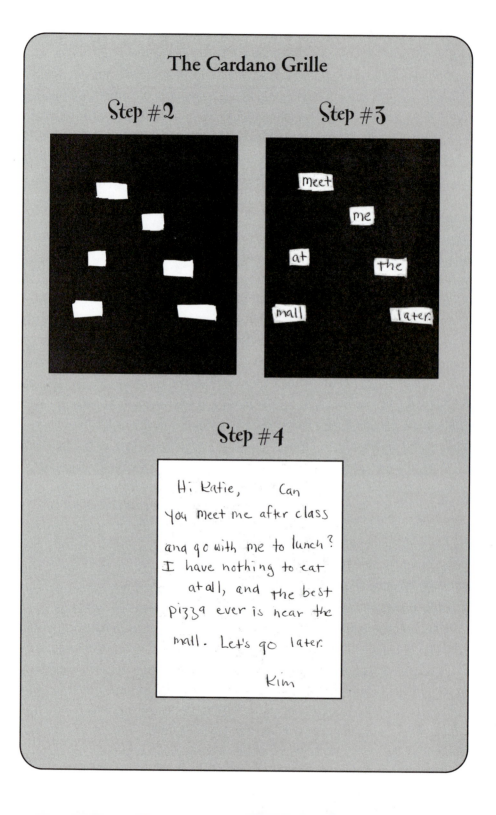

The American Revolution

On July 4, 1776, the American colonies made their Declaration of Independence. The desire for freedom from British rule had been growing for a number of years. During the Boston Tea Party, colonists dumped tea off a merchant vessel to protest what they considered unfair taxes. The British Parliament passed laws that the colonists called the Intolerable Acts, demanding repayment. One thing led to another until the colonists and the British met in the first battle of the war at Bunker Hill, Massachusetts.

The colonists who supported independence were Patriots. Their army was the Continental Army led by General George Washington. Other colonists, the Tories, remained loyal to the British. At first, it seemed the British would win the war. They captured New York and Philadelphia. The Continental Army was not well supplied, and during the harsh winters many soldiers got sick and died, and others deserted. But most would not give up the fight for freedom.

General Washington wanted the support of other countries in Europe. Benjamin Franklin went abroad to convince them to help. Finally France, then Spain and others, joined the Patriots' side.

Women helped on the battlefield. Many got the nickname "Molly Pitcher" for bringing pitchers of water to wounded soldiers. A few wanted to fight, but they had to disguise themselves as men to do so. Those who stayed home knitted socks and made shirts for the soldiers. They even melted pewter dishes to make bullets. And they spied, sometimes taking secret messages directly to the army camps.

In 1781, after six years of fighting, the British surrendered in Yorktown, Virginia. The colonies adopted the Constitution, and with the words "We the People of the United States," a new nation was created.

LYDIA DARRAGH

The Fighting Quaker

1729–1789

*L*ydia tossed and turned in her bed. She desperately wanted to know what the British officers were discussing downstairs. But what if they caught her eavesdropping? Finally, she could take it no longer. She got out of bed, crept down to the parlor, and put her ear to the keyhole. Her heart beat so loudly she thought they'd hear it through the door as she listened to plans for a surprise attack on General Washington and his troops.

Lydia hurried back to bed but there was no sleep for her that night. She had to get the information to General Washington. Her son Charles was serving with him. What would happen to him if the British sneaked into their camp? How would she get the message through without getting caught?

* * * *

Lydia Barrington was born in 1729 in Dublin, Ireland. At the age of twenty-four, she married a teacher, William Darragh, and soon after they set sail for America. Lydia worked to help support her growing family. She was at various times a midwife, a nurse, and even a mortician. She lived in Philadelphia, where the Declaration of Independence was drafted in 1776, and she believed deeply in independence for the colonies.

When the British invaded Philadelphia, British officers used Lydia's parlor as a regular meeting place to discuss war strategies. Lydia and her family were Quakers, and since most Quakers didn't believe in fighting or taking sides during wartime, the British thought they were safe from American spies. They couldn't imagine that Lydia was a spy, or that her oldest son had joined General Washington's army.

Whenever Lydia heard any useful information, she sent it on to Charles. The night Lydia heard about the British plans for a surprise attack, she knew it was news she had to deliver personally. Early the next morning she bundled up in her warmest clothes. Putting her wool cloak over her shoulders, she told her husband that she was going to get flour.

The Frankford Mill was a ways out of town, but women could get a pass to leave the city when they needed flour. Her husband suggested she send their household helper instead, but Lydia said no. She couldn't tell him why she was the one who had to go. If she got caught and the British questioned him, she wanted him to be able to say truthfully he didn't know anything about it. The British hanged spies they discovered.

Lydia took a flour sack and set out over the icy streets. She didn't know how far she'd have to travel. It all depended on if she came across someone she could trust. Sometimes General Washington's soldiers rode about the countryside on horseback to get news from spies. If Lydia didn't meet up with anyone, she was ready to walk the entire twelve miles to General Washington's camp.

Lydia dropped the empty flour sack off at the mill, telling the miller she'd be back later to pick up the flour. Then she headed for an inn where spies sometimes met. As she tramped along the road, one of General Washington's officers rode up. Luckily, he was a friend of Lydia's. Quickly, Lydia gave him the information and he rode off to warn General Washington. Lydia hurried back to the mill for the flour. The British would be less likely to suspect her of anything if she got home before dark.

Because of Lydia's actions, General Washington's troops were ready for the British's surprise attack. After three days of intense fighting, the British gave up and retreated to Philadelphia, where they spent the rest of the winter.

Lydia was relieved that the battle had gone well, but now she had another worry. What if the British found out what she had done?

Back in Philadelphia, the British officers summoned Lydia and expressed their surprise that information discussed only in her house had gotten through to General Washington. One of the officers thought she had been asleep the night they were there. He looked her right in the eye and asked her if anyone else in the house could have overheard them talking. She was able to say no without flinching, for she was the only one who had been up that night. They were puzzled, but they did not question her further.

That spring the British finally left Philadelphia. Lydia continued to help the Revolution by nursing the wounded in the surrounding countryside.

Sadly, Lydia was banned from Quaker meetings for a while for getting involved in the war and for her role as a spy. But that didn't stop her from doing what she thought was right. She was later forgiven by her Quaker community, and when she died she was laid to rest in a Quaker burial ground. Her local newspaper praised her for "her many contributions to her community's health and welfare."[1]

Spy Trivia

During the American Revolution, coded messages were wrapped around buttons and covered with cloth that matched the jacket they were sewn onto. Sometimes Lydia Darragh hid messages in her younger son John's buttons so he could sneak them to his brother Charles at Washington's camp.

ANNA SMITH STRONG

Spy in Petticoats

1740 – 1812

If the British were watching her, Anna hoped they would think she was just hanging her wash out to dry that sunny morning on Long Island, New York. Besides, how could a petticoat on a clothesline be a secret signal? But Anna's petticoat was!

* * * *

Anna Smith was born on April 14, 1740 in the manor house her great-grandfather had built on Long Island when he arrived in the colonies. When she was twenty years old, she married Selah Strong and they settled down in the manor.

Many of Anna's wealthy relatives were Tories, but Anna and Selah were Patriots. Anna's husband fought against the British when the revolution broke out. He was arrested and held in a British prison ship.

When the British invaded Long Island, they took over Anna's family's manor house, so Anna sent her young children to Connecticut, which was still in Patriot hands. She stayed on Long Island because she was a spy.

Anna was part of a spy ring started at General Washington's request. Most of the spies in the ring were her childhood friends. She knew she could trust them. If only she could keep the British from being suspicious of her.

About once a week, one of the spies galloped to New York City to dig up information about the British troops. Upon his return, he would hide the message in a drop-box on Anna's friend Abraham Woodhull's farm, across the bay from her. Meanwhile, Anna waited for word from another spy, Caleb Brewster, who was a whaleboat captain. He would slip past the British ships and hide in one of the coves in the bay.

Whenever Anna found out where Caleb was, she hung out her black petticoat. The spies had given all the coves a number, so beside the petticoat she hung up the corresponding number of handkerchiefs. Three handkerchiefs meant "go to cove number 3." Abraham would count Anna's handkerchiefs and know right where to find Caleb. After dark, he would sneak across the fields to the cove. Once Caleb got the message, he rowed over to Connecticut. From there the message went straight to General Washington.

One day the British got hold of a letter General Washington had written about a new spy in the ring. Luckily for Anna, all the names of the spies were in code. The British doubled their efforts to find the spies. They were already suspicious of Abraham and they were always on the lookout for Caleb's whaleboat.

Anna refused to flee to Connecticut and pushed aside her fears of getting caught. Without her clothesline signals, Abraham would have trouble finding Caleb. That would give the British a chance to follow him and catch him with the secret messages.

After the war, Anna was reunited with her husband and their children. They moved back to the manor. Years later, Anna had the honor of meeting General Washington, president of her new nation, the nation she had risked her life to help create.

SPY SECRETS:
A Dead Drop

When undercover agents meet each other to exchange information, it can be dangerous. Someone might see them. So many spies hide messages in prearranged secret places called dead drops. A dead drop can be a hollowed-out rock or log or just an unexpected place, like the pages of a book in a library.

To make your own dead drop, mold papier-mâché or craft clay into the shape of a rock to hide outside. Make sure to leave part of the inside hollowed out for the message.

Let the dead drop dry and then paint or decorate it to fit in where you plan to hide it. Insert your message. Will it be written in code? Once the dead drop is in place, give a friend the prearranged signal that there's an important message waiting for her. How quickly can she find and read the message?

EMILY GEIGER

Caught!

---

c. 1763 – ?

Emily knew she couldn't outrun the Tory scouts who blocked her way. So she pulled up her horse and answered their questions. When she told them she lived on Cedar Creek, they accused her of being a spy. They knew she wasn't just out for a ride, since she was almost twenty miles from home.

They locked her in a barn and went to get a woman friend of theirs to search her. Emily paced back and forth. The message she carried was sure to be found!

* * * *

Emily Geiger was born about 1763 in the Fairfield District of South Carolina. Her father was a well-to-do plantation owner. Emily and her family were Patriots. Many of the residents of the area were Tories. It seemed everyone was spying on everyone else.

Eighteen-year-old Emily kept up with all the war news, even though her father was too old to fight. The war in the southern colonies was going badly. Patriot General Nathanael Greene and his troops had attacked the British at Fort Ninety-Six, but the British were too strong for them and they had had to retreat. After marching for several days, General Greene set up camp near Emily's plantation.

One of the Patriots talked to Emily's father. General Greene was looking for a fresh horse so he could send a message to General Sumter, who was camped farther east. The British were on the move again and the Patriots had to try to stop them.

Emily was tired of hearing all the bad news. She wanted to do something to help. She knew the area so well she felt she could ride through it blindfolded. She could surely take the message faster than any of General Greene's soldiers.

Reluctantly, her father agreed and Emily galloped to Greene's camp. He must have been shocked when he discovered she wasn't bringing him the horse but was offering to take the message herself. He didn't want to send her into danger. Tories would be patrolling the area, on the lookout for anyone heading toward General Sumter's camp.

Emily laid out her plan. She knew the roads well and she had family nearby. It would be easier for a young girl to get through than for a Patriot soldier.

Her confidence convinced General Greene she could do it. Hurriedly, he wrote down the message. No matter what happened, he warned her, the enemy must not get the information. He couldn't protect her if she was caught.

Emily rode more than halfway to the camp when the Tories stopped her and locked her in the barn. Trapped, Emily peeked through a crack in the barn door. A Tory woman was coming across the field right toward her. She would soon be searched. There was only one thing to do.

Emily read over the letter, quickly memorized it, then tore it up. Piece by piece she ate it. When the woman arrived to search her, nothing could be found.

Emily was soon back on the road. The next time she was stopped, it was by General Sumter's men. She boldly relayed the message to them. As she and her horse rested, the soldiers prepared to meet the British.

Emily watched them with pride, knowing she too had served the cause of liberty.

PATIENCE LOVELL WRIGHT

Artist and Spy
1725 – 1786

Trouble awaited Patience Wright one evening as she walked through Paris. She was stopped by guards who demanded to see what was in the bundle under her arm. She was furious. Her olive-green eyes flashed as she loudly protested. The guards insisted that she open the bundle. They stepped back in horror. Inside was a human head!

Patience did not speak French and could not understand their conversation, but she could see they were intent on arresting her. She repeated the name of the hotel where she was staying, Hotel d'York, until they took her there. A friend at the hotel explained that Patience was an artist.

How the officers laughed when they discovered the head was one of her wax-work figures! But Patience had another use for her artwork. Her hollowed-out wax busts concealed secret messages. She was a spy for America.

* * * *

Patience Lovell was born on Long Island, New York, in 1725. Her family moved to a small town in New Jersey when Patience was four years old. Her father had some odd ideas. He insisted that the entire family dress in pure white clothing to symbolize their innocence and cleanliness. What a sight: Patience and her eight sisters wearing white flowing dresses, white veils, white straw hats, and white wooden shoes! The girls put color into their lives in other ways. They played with clay and flour dough, sculpting miniature figures and painting them in bright clothes.

Patience couldn't wait to grow up. She was a free spirit and liked traveling. She made friends easily wherever she went. When she was old enough, she left home for the big city of Philadelphia, about twenty miles away. She tried to make a living as a clay modeler, but she didn't have much success.

At the age of twenty-three, Patience married Joseph Wright and they settled in her hometown to raise a family. Patience was left to provide for her young children when Joseph died. Her sister, Rachel, also a widow, had a great idea. Waxwork shows were popular throughout the colonies. Why not try their hand at wax figures? The sisters agreed to start a waxworks business, which turned into a great success. They each established galleries—Rachel in Philadelphia, Patience in New York City.

Patience made busts of several well-known American statesmen. While she was traveling in Boston, she met Ben Franklin's favorite sister, Jane Mecom. Jane offered to write a letter to introduce Patience to her brother, who was in London. He could introduce Patience to famous people there who might pose for her.

So Patience set sail for London, and met Ben Franklin when she arrived. Patience had a surprise for him, a little trick she had perfected in New York City. As she sat chatting, she worked with her hands hidden under her apron to shape the head of her host. Ben was startled to see a perfect replica of himself when she revealed it to him. He was amazed by her talent.

Patience settled in the posh section of London near Buckingham Palace. She opened her doors and men and women of society came, in their glittering waistcoats and velvet gowns. Patience wore her plain homespun dress, but she was bold and brash. The British flipped for her. Over and over she told the story of the nine little girls in white growing up in New Jersey. Her waxwork was praised in London newspapers. Lords and Earls sat for her. Even the king and queen sat for her, and she insisted on calling them George and Charlotte!

Then the Boston Tea Party took place across the ocean. Patience listened to the British Lords pass the "Intolerable Acts." People in England were divided. Many felt the punishment for the colonists was too harsh. Others felt the opposition in America had to be crushed.

Patience sent letters to leaders in the colonies, telling them which people in London they could trust and what the British military was planning. When she discovered her letters were being intercepted, she devised another way to send news—tucked into the hollowed-out wax busts she sent to her sister's gallery in Philadelphia.

While in England, Patience took every opportunity to speak out for American independence and to encourage those back in the colonies to fight what she considered to be British oppression. When she heard about the battles in Massachusetts at the start of the Revolution, she marched down to the palace and scolded the king!

At this time there were many rumors of plots against the king. Some Americans had been imprisoned in the Tower of London. Patience worked for their release, and she gave refuge to prisoners who escaped, helping them get to safety in France.

When the colonists in America started winning battles, Patience continued to speak out. She was threatened by the king's men and went to France for awhile in order to gain safety.

Patience was back in England when the war ended. Her son Joseph, who was also an artist, went back to America to do a portrait of the triumphant General Washington. Patience, now in her sixties, began making plans to return to America, but she fell before she could go and died from injury-related complications.

If she had returned, Patience surely would have met General Washington. When she had written to Washington to thank him for sitting for her son, he had replied back: "I should be proud to see a person so universally celebrated; and on whom Nature has bestowed such rare and uncommon gifts."[1]

LAODICEA SPRINGFIELD

Daring Dicey

1766 – 1837

Dicey didn't dare ask anyone for help. Her father had already warned her to be extra careful after some of their neighbors saw her spying on the British. But she had to do something to warn her brother when she learned the settlement where he lived would soon be attacked.

Dicey did dare to go by herself. Later that night when everyone was asleep, she sneaked out of the house and headed for the river. She plunged into the rough water, swift and swollen from recent rainstorms, and barely made it across. Dripping wet, she hurried on and reached her brother before dawn. She warmed herself by his fire, then quickly headed back home, hoping her brother and his friends would get away in time.

* * * *

Dicey was the nickname of Laodicea Langston. She was born May 14, 1766, to Solomon and Sarah Langston, who owned a plantation in South Carolina. Dicey's parents were Patriots. The Langston family prospered by working hard raising and harvesting crops. Dicey was strong and spunky. She worked alongside her older brother on the plantation for most of her sixteen years and she missed him enormously after he joined a company of Patriot fighters.

Dicey's neighbors were almost equally split between Patriots and Tories. The British were being beaten by General Washington's army in the northern colonies, so they turned their attention to the southern colonies and won many battles. Patriot soldiers roamed the countryside in small bands like the one Dicey's brother joined. They would not let go of freedom without a fight.

The Bloody Scout was the name for a group of Tories known to be especially cruel to the Patriots. They were also the ones who planned to attack the settlement where Dicey's brother lived. They'd threatened Dicey once before. After her nighttime trip to warn her brother, they paid her father a visit. Dicey heard them shouting as she came in from the fields. They said they'd shoot her father on the spot if he didn't tell them what he knew. Dicey ran to him and threw her arms around him. She told the men they'd have to shoot her first.

Suddenly one man pushed the gun aside and told them not to shoot. The men left without harming Dicey or her father. The Bloody Scout had an agreement among them. They would show mercy if one of them asked for his neighbors or relatives to be spared. That day the Langstons were lucky.

Dicey's bravery didn't stop there. On another occasion, her brother sent his friends for a musket he had hidden at home. He told Dicey to ask them for a sign so she'd know it was them. When they arrived, Dicey ran to get the musket. Only when she brought it out did she realized she'd forgotten to ask for the sign. Immediately, she demanded it but one of the men just laughed—he had no need for a sign, for there was the musket.

Dicey pointed it right at him, daring him to take it. He quickly gave the sign, admiring her nerve. Several years later, this young man, Thomas Springfield, returned to ask Dicey to be his wife. After the war, they settled in the area and raised 22 children and 140 grandchildren and great-grandchildren.

When Dicey died, the newspaper praised her for her "many daring deeds on behalf of her suffering country and friends."[1]

The Wars of Independence in Spanish America

Spaniards settled in the Americas during the same time the British colonized North America. The king of Spain appointed a viceroy, or governor, to rule each of his colonies. Though the colonies were independent of each other, their social structure was similar. In every colony, Spanish-born citizens had the most privileges and held the highest offices. Creoles (people who had Spanish ancestors but were born in the colonies) and the native people felt they were second-class citizens. They studied the freedom movements in the United States and France. They too wanted independence.

The year 1810 marked the start of many uprisings throughout the Spanish colonies. In Mexico (then part of New Spain), Padre Hidalgo raised the famous *grito* (the cry for freedom) on September 16, 1810. Though he and other leaders of the revolution were executed, those fighting for independence would not give up. In 1821, after years of struggle, Mexico became independent from Spain.

The independence movement in Colombia began on July 20, 1810, with Creole and native demands that the viceroy step down. A civil war followed over who would govern Colombia (then part of New Granada). Finally, the revolutionaries united to defeat the Spanish forces on August 7, 1819, and Colombia gained its independence.

Women did their part. They helped support families whose sons and fathers were fighting. They raised money, and wealthy Creole women even spent their own fortunes to buy supplies for revolutionary soldiers. Some women spied, and some had to go into hiding in the hills because of their beliefs. Women were not afraid to die to win freedom for others.

JOSEFA ORTIZ DE DOMINGUEZ

La Heroina

1768 – 1829

The lock clicked. Josefa's skirts swished as she marched across the room to look out the window. As soon as her husband left the house, Josefa called to the guard, who supported the revolutionaries as she did. Being locked in her room was not going to stop her from warning the revolutionary leader, Padre Hidalgo, that the Spanish authorities were looking for him.

Josefa's husband was the corregidor, the top royal official in town. He was ordered to conduct a search for Hidalgo and other revolutionaries. He sympathized with them, but he wanted to stay on the good side of the viceroy. And he wanted to keep his wife safe.

Josefa, however, wasn't worried about her own safety. She would do anything to help the poor of Mexico be free from Spanish oppression. Through the keyhole, Josefa urged the guard to warn Hidalgo with the news. But when the guard reached Hidalgo, the revolutionary leader refused to go into hiding. Instead he rang the church bells in his parish, calling the people to start the revolution against Spain.

* * * *

Josefa Ortiz was born in a small town outside Mexico City in 1768. Her family was Creole. Josefa's parents died when she was very young. She grew up in an orphanage in Mexico City. She had to work for her education, and she made the most of it.

When Josefa graduated from college, she married Miguel Dominguez, a young lawyer she had met when he visited the school on business. When he was appointed corregidor, Josefa was suddenly at the center of social and cultural activities. But she didn't sit back and enjoy a privileged life. She had washed dishes and scrubbed floors at school. She knew what it was to be poor, and she knew the laws in the country were unjust.

Josefa joined other leaders and intellectuals who were dissatisfied with Spanish rule. They met in secret to discuss how to fight for freedom. Many Mexicans longed to be free from Spanish rule. They put their hopes in Padre Hidalgo and his uprising.

Several days after Josefa's warning to Hidalgo, she and her husband were arrested. Leading citizens came to their defense until they were released. Josefa, though closely watched, refused to stop working for the revolutionaries and started spying as a way to stand up for her beliefs.

Josefa hadn't learned how to write in school. In Mexico girls were taught to read, but there was a notion that if they could write as well, they would waste time sending long love letters to their boyfriends. Josefa sent the revolutionaries information about government activities the way people today write anonymous letters. She cut words out of publications and pasted them together. She rolled up the notes and wrapped them around firecrackers. No one thought to inspect them for secret messages.

Josefa convinced townspeople and even soldiers in the viceroy's army to join the independence movement. She gave money to aid the revolutionaries and once again fell under suspicion. The viceroy sent an official to question her. Leave it to Josefa. She didn't pass up any chance to spread her beliefs. The official reported back to the viceroy that Josefa had even tried to recruit him!

This time when Josefa was arrested, she went straight to prison. As she was led through the streets she reprimanded the soldiers. "So many soldiers to guard one poor woman? Well, with my blood I will create an inheritance for my sons."[1]

Josefa did not have to shed her blood. She was not executed, but she was placed in solitary confinement, because she would not stop giving speeches to everyone around her.

Eventually, Josefa was let out of prison to care for her ailing husband. A new viceroy offered peace to the revolutionaries, letting them take over the government. Josefa did not wholeheartedly approve of what was happening. She accused some of the revolutionaries-turned-rulers of gaining power for themselves and ignoring the poor, for whom the war had been started.

Years later, Josefa was honored by the Mexican state legislature for her role in the struggle for independence. Today a glorious statue of her resides in the Plaza de Santo Domingo in Mexico City, commemorating her work.

SPY SECRETS:
A Greek Skytale

Ancient Greeks invented the "skytale" (rhymes with Italy), which was a stick wrapped with narrow strips of papyrus, leather, or parchment. The message was written on the wrapping, then the strip was removed and passed to the messenger. Only when it was rewound around a stick with the exact same diameter as the skytale could the message be deciphered.

To Make a Skytale

1. Choose a rounded stick like a wooden dowel, broomstick handle, or even a paper towel roll.

2. Cut two to three one-inch wide strips of plain 8.5" x 11" paper and tape them together to form one long strip.

3. Tape one end of the strip at a diagonal at the top of the stick and wind the rest down in a spiral. Tape the other end down.

4. Write a message down the stick vertically, placing one or two letters on each piece of paper.

5. Unwind the paper and give it to a friend with instructions on how to decipher your message. Be sure to tell him or her the exact diameter of your skytale.

LEONA VICARIO ROO

Madre de la Patria

1789 – 1842

The Mass ended and Leona and two of her friends left the church. It was a pleasant day, so they strolled to the marketplace where vendors sold fresh fruits, vegetables, and brightly-colored dahlias. Suddenly a woman none of them knew stepped into their path and handed Leona a note. She disappeared as quickly as she had come.

Leona's heart pounded as she read the message: "The courier is in jail. The authorities are looking for you." [1]

Her spying had been discovered! She managed to stay calm and continued walking with her friends. A short distance away, she hailed a coach and asked to be taken to a small village on the outskirts of Mexico City. From there, she walked to another village. For the next three days she moved from house to house, while her friends in Mexico City were questioned as to her whereabouts.

Knowing she could not go back, Leona found someone to guide her and set out for the camp of the revolutionaries, hidden in the surrounding hills. There she would be safe.

* * * *

Leona Vicario was born in Mexico City on April 10, 1789, to wealthy Spanish-born parents. They were well educated and made sure their daughter received good schooling, even though at that time girls in Mexico often only received religious training.

Leona was not just beautiful; she was smart too. She studied classical literature, the history of Mexico, natural sciences, philosophy, French, music, drawing, and painting. Many intellectuals in Mexico discussed how citizens in other countries fought for their freedom, and Leona soon came to support Mexico's revolution against Spanish rule.

When Leona was only eighteen years old, her parents died suddenly and one of her uncles became her guardian. He helped her set up a home of her own and let her control the substantial fortune her parents had left her. She met a young lawyer named Andrés Quintana Roo at her uncle's law firm. Andrés shared Leona's beliefs about the revolution. When he asked Leona to marry him, her uncle, who was against the revolution, refused to give his consent. Leona bowed to her uncle's wishes, and Andrés left Mexico City to work for the revolutionaries.

Leona encouraged others to join the revolution, saying she wished she were a man so she could fight with them. She organized all the best arms makers in Mexico City to journey to Campo de Gallo, where the revolutionaries were hiding. This was a huge blow to the Spanish government and a great help to the revolution. Leona paid for weapons and other resources. She believed so deeply in the cause of freedom that when her money was gone, she began selling her silver, jewelry, and furniture.

Leona also set up a spy ring, sending couriers to rebel camps with information about what the government in Mexico City was doing and where their troops were being dispatched. "Enriqueta" was Leona's code name, and she used other code names for other revolutionaries. But when one courier was intercepted, government officials figured out it was Leona who sent the message. They were planning to arrest her the day she received the warning. The day after her daring escape from Mexico City, she was declared guilty of treason.

Because her uncle was loyal to the government, he convinced the officials to give Leona a pardon. He sent out a search party to find her. At first she refused his help, but she wasn't used to life on the run. She eventually returned to Mexico City. When she wouldn't cooperate with the government officials, they arrested her. No matter how much they threatened her, she wouldn't reveal the names of other revolutionaries.

After she had spent forty-two days in prison, Leona's friends and family helped her escape. She hid in the surrounding neighborhood. Dressed as a ragged mule driver, her face streaked with dirt, she escaped from the city again.

She met up with Andrés, and this time when he asked her to marry him, she accepted. Many of the leaders of the independence movement were caught and executed, and Leona and Andrés spent several more years in hiding. Their first daughter was born in a cave in the hills. They kept speaking out in favor of independence and freedom for the poor, refusing all offers of pardon from the government.

When the revolution finally ended, Leona dedicated herself to the care and education of her two daughters. She wished to receive no special honors, saying her service was nothing out of the ordinary. But she has been honored throughout Mexico. At the time of her death, the government newspaper called Leona *Madre de la Patria,* mother of her country.

POLICARPA SALAVARRIETA

La Pola

1795 – 1817

The soldiers closed in around La Pola. She had been caught at last. Her thoughts were not on her tragedy but on the papers hidden in the kitchen—papers filled with the names of all the others in her spy ring. How could she destroy them before the soldiers began searching the house?

La Pola started shouting at the soldiers, calling them cowards and praising the revolutionaries. She turned to Andrea, the young mother who owned the house, and said that the baby needed to be fed. Andrea immediately understood what La Pola wanted her to do. Andrea hurried to the kitchen, and La Pola kept the soldiers distracted with her ranting and raving. Soon all the papers were burning in the kitchen fireplace.

* * * *

La Pola was the nickname of Policarpa Salavarrieta. She was born on January 26, 1795, into a Creole family in Colombia. She grew up in Guaduas, a stopover on a major route between the coast and Santafé de Bogotá, the capital where the viceroy lived. Her father was a merchant, and the family lived two blocks from the central plaza—a perfect spot to hear news carried by the travelers. La Pola often knew what was happening in the outlying areas before the viceroy did.

The young girl was at the center of it all. She listened to the grumblings of Creoles who were tired of being under Spanish rule. Two of her older brothers were Augustinian monks. The head of their monastery was a staunch believer in freedom for the colonies from Spain. La Pola read all the pamphlets he wrote in support of a revolution.

She was fifteen years old when the Creoles took over the government. Some Creoles were loyalists who still wanted Spanish rule. La Pola cheered the revolutionaries who marched through the streets, wishing she could join them. She was full of courage and always ready to speak out. La Pola talked young men into joining the battle for freedom. She helped families whose sons were fighting. When revolutionaries captured by the loyalist soldiers were chained together and paraded through the village, she gave them sips of lemonade or coconut soup.

More important, La Pola became a spy. She was a seamstress and worked for wealthy Spaniards, making their clothing in their homes. She eavesdropped on all their conversations and learned where the Spanish troops were moving and what they were planning next.

The Spanish troops managed to retake the government, and a reign of terror began. Revolutionaries and anyone suspected of supporting their cause were executed. Many who were opposed to Spanish rule now fell silent, but not La Pola. Her views were well known, so to be on the safe side, she moved away. Friends arranged for her to live with Andrea Ricaurte, the wife of a revolutionary.

La Pola was part of an underground organization led by the wealthy Almeyda brothers, who supplied money and arms to the revolutionaries. More and more young men were joining in the fight. They escaped into the *llanos*, the grasslands beyond the city, using a network of safe houses La Pola had set up.

Then one of the Almeydas' contacts turned traitor and revealed their identities. The Almeydas were imprisoned, but that didn't stop La Pola. She continued sending messages and supplies to the revolutionary camps. Then a courier was caught carrying a note from her. The Spanish authorities found out who she was and began a relentless search for her.

La Pola was not ready to go into hiding. Not yet. She had one more escape to plan. With her help, the Almeyda brothers broke out of jail and disappeared into the *llanos*.

A few days later, one of the shopkeepers she knew took a bribe and betrayed her. Soldiers burst into Andrea's home. La Pola was taken to jail. She could save herself—all she had to do was give up the names of others and she could go free.

She refused. And she refused to be silenced in her support of the revolution. Even as La Pola was led through the streets to her execution she cried out: "Although I am a woman and young, I have more than enough courage to suffer this death and a thousand more. Do not forget my example."[1]

People did not forget her example. Many others lost their lives fighting for independence in Colombia. But independence came. Today La Pola is honored as a national heroine.

Spy File:
Your Family Story

What do you know about the women in your family? Many women's stories are lost because they don't think what they've done is important enough to record.

Talk to your mother, aunts, and grandmothers about courage—the kind of courage the girls and women in this book displayed. Ask about the kind of courage they had to show at home, in school, at work, or in special circumstances in their lives. Ask them what they remember about their grandmothers and great-grandmothers.

Write down their stories, filling in the information about birth-dates and places and parents, what they studied in school, where and when they graduated, if and when they got married, and what children they had. Add photographs and keepsakes.

You may be surprised to find some famous heroines in your own family.

The Civil War

The Civil War officially started on April 12, 1861, when the Confederate forces fired on the Union-held Fort Sumter, South Carolina. But unrest had been growing in the United States for years over the issue of slavery. While there were no laws against slavery, more and more people were speaking out and acting out against it.

When Abraham Lincoln was elected president, many Southern states thought slavery would soon be outlawed. They wanted each state to have the right to choose how to handle it. Eleven states voted to secede from (to leave) the Union. Together they formed the Confederate States of America and elected Jefferson Davis as their president. The Confederate White House was set up in Richmond, Virginia. The remaining states in the United States went to war against the Confederacy under the claim that it was illegal for states to secede.

Women were active in all aspects of the war. A few marched on the battlefields as flag bearers, but those who wanted to fight had to disguise themselves as men. Men thought women shouldn't even be on the battlefields as nurses, but women insisted. At home, women gathered together to roll bandages and pack baskets of food for the soldiers. A few women became famous as spies. Many others, including slave women, worked unofficially, spying and sneaking into camps to tell the soldiers what the enemy was up to.

For four years war raged between the states. Almost as many American lives were lost in the Civil War as in all the other wars in which America has fought. Finally, the Union forces captured Richmond and on April 9, 1865, the Confederates surrendered. The United States of America was united once more.

HARRIET TUBMAN

Without Equal

c. 1820 – 1913

Harriet tied the scarf under her chin and shuffled along the dirt road-way. She looked just like an old slave woman taking the chickens to market. Along the way, she whispered to the slaves she met. Tonight she would be wait-ing in the woods to lead slaves out of the South to the North.

As she turned a corner, she sucked in her breath. Her former master was coming toward her. He might see through her disguise! She had to get away from him. Quickly she loosed the cords that held the chickens. He laughed as the squawking chickens flew over a fence, but he kept on walking when Harriet chased after them, stumbling and waving her arms.

Harriet got the last laugh. That night, several slaves escaped with her to freedom in the North.

* * * *

Harriet Ross was born on the eastern shore of Maryland around 1820. Her parents, Harriet and Benjamin Ross, told her stories of their past life in West Africa. They were from the Ashanti tribe of warriors. Harriet saw that warrior spirit in herself.

Her cradle name was Arminta, Minty for short. Eventually, she changed her name to Harriet after her mother. It wasn't legal for slaves to go to school, so Harriet never learned to read or write. Harriet's owner, Mr.

Brodas, hired out his slaves to work on his neighbor's plantations. From the time she was five or six years old, she lived on other nearby plantations, working long hours even though she was very young.

One time when Harriet was setting the table, she reached for a taste of sugar when her mistress's back was turned. She'd never had it before, and it looked so good. Her mistress caught her and beat her so hard that she spent weeks at home under her mother's gentle care. Harriet got a reputation as being uncooperative. Other mistresses didn't want to hire her, so she was sent into the fields. She was only five feet tall, but she developed strength driving oxen and splitting logs to make fence rails. Harriet often worked side by side with her father, who showed her the North Star and told her how to use it like a compass so she'd never get lost.

When she was about fifteen years old, Harriet tried to protect a slave from a beating. As the slave broke free, the overseer threw a heavy lead weight at him and hit Harriet's forehead instead. She was in a coma for weeks, and for the rest of her life she was subject to sudden blackouts and severe headaches. As Harriet recovered, once again under her mother's care, she began to think about the nature of slavery. Didn't slaves have the right to liberty too?

Harriet married a free black man, John Tubman. Even though Harriet's husband was free, he thought Harriet got too upset about being a slave. He even threatened to turn her in if she attempted to run away. When Harriet eventually escaped, he wanted nothing to do with her.

Harriet didn't stop thinking about the injustice of slavery. When she heard that two of her sisters were about to be sold to plantations in the deep South, her heart sank. She couldn't help them—they were already in chains. That day, she convinced her brothers to run away with her. Tramping through the cypress swamp in the dark of night, her brothers worried that they'd never make it, that they'd end up getting lost or being caught by the overseer and get a terrible beating. Eventually her brothers stopped and refused to walk any further. Harriet went back to the Brodas plantation with them.

But when she crept back into bed that night, she knew next time she wouldn't give up. Next time she'd go alone. Two days later, as darkness fell, Harriet set out on the path she would take many more times over the years, leading other slaves to freedom. After hiding during the days and trudging night after night, she finally stood on free soil in Pennsylvania. "I looked at my hands," she recalled later, "to see if I was the same person now that I was free." As the sun warmed the fields she thought it was how heaven must feel.[1]

Soon after that, Harriet started the work she was most famous for, being a conductor on the Underground Railroad, the secret network of people who helped slaves escape to freedom in the North. Later, when the Civil War began, Harriet had another mission: to be a spy.

Over a ten-year period, Harriet led some 300 slaves to freedom. No one who went with her ever got lost. Between trips, she supported herself as a cook and a maid in local hotels. She brought her entire family to freedom, including her two sisters. Her mother and father settled with her in Auburn, New York.

A reward of $40,000 was offered for Harriet's capture. When war broke out, her friends hurried her off to Canada. Unable to stay hidden when there was work to be done, Harriet went to South Carolina to assist blacks who sought refuge with the Union forces. As the war progressed, the Union officers needed information. They knew about Harriet's work slipping secretly through the countryside on the Underground Railroad. Could she help them now?

Harriet organized a small band of black men to act as scouts, searching out where the enemy stored food, ammunition, and livestock and reporting on the location of troops. For two years she spied on the Confederates. She also led a famous raid on South Carolina's Combahee River. In several gunboats, she and Union soldiers headed upriver to destroy bridges and ammunition. On the way back, the gunboats picked up 750 slaves along the riverbank and carried them to freedom.

Harriet's old head injuries started causing her serious problems, and she returned to her home in Auburn for a while. Not too long after that, she was on her way back to South Carolina when the war ended. Weeks later, while boarding a train to go back to Auburn, she was yanked off the coach and tossed into the baggage car. It seemed the idea of equality for blacks had not gotten through to everyone.

After the war, Harriet supported herself and her parents by working in her garden and selling vegetables and apples. She raised funds to start schools for blacks in the south. She married Nelson Davis but kept her famous surname, Tubman.

Harriet gave speeches for women's rights with Susan B. Anthony and other suffragists. She believed that no one—woman or man, black or white—would be truly free until everyone was free. She nursed sick neighbors and eventually started a home for aged and impoverished blacks. She moved into it herself a few years before her death.

England's Queen Victoria read a biography of Harriet. The Queen was so impressed she sent Harriet a silver medal, which Harriet treasured. Harriet was not awarded any honors by the U.S. government for her service, but local Civil War veterans led a military service for her when she died. A bugler played Taps (a melody traditionally played at official military funerals) for this woman they so admired.

After her death, William Still, an antislavery activist who worked with Harriet on the Underground Railroad, wrote of her courage, her cunning, and her tireless work: "She was without equal."[2]

SPY SECRETS:
Freedom Quilts

The Underground Railroad was a secret network of people who helped slaves escape to freedom. The movement actually started soon after slaves arrived in the colonies and was a more organized network in the 1800s, especially during the time leading up to the Civil War, when slaves in the South were heading for northern states or Canada.

There were safe houses all along the many routes leading north. The owners of these houses were willing to shelter runaway slaves. Signs marked the safe houses: a lantern hung on a hitching post, a quilt draped on a porch or used as a window cover. These quilts were later referred to as freedom quilts.

ELIZABETH VAN LEW

"Crazy Bet"

1818 – 1900

The coded message was ready. "Crazy Bet" hid it in her basket and headed for the marketplace, humming in her crazy way. Hiding behind a silly smile, she scanned the crowd, looking for one of the spies she knew who could take the secret message to the Union officers.

Suddenly a strange man whispered in her ear as he passed: "I'm going through tonight!"

"Crazy Bet" quickened her pace to catch up with him. She wondered if she should slip him the message. Then she wondered if he really was a spy for the Union. He might be a Confederate detective. They were swarming around the city looking for spies.

As she glanced at the man's face, something told her to keep walking. She hurried home, hoping she could find another way to send the message on.[1]

* * * *

"Crazy Bet" is what people started calling her, but her name was Elizabeth Van Lew. She was born into one of Richmond, Virginia's wealthiest families on October 15, 1818. Her father owned a successful hardware business. Her mother came from a wealthy family in Philadelphia, where her grandfather was once the mayor.

The Van Lews lived in a huge mansion and kept a staff of slaves. They entertained famous people, including poets and politicians. Jefferson Davis, the man who became the president of the Confederacy, was a frequent guest in their home.

Elizabeth was as delicate as a china doll. Curly blonde hair framed her face. When she was seven years old she went away to her mother's former school in Philadelphia where Northern attitudes against slavery were strong. Elizabeth was the kind of girl who thought things through for herself. It didn't matter if she was from the South, she realized, because she did not believe in slavery either. After she finished her studies and returned home, she dared to speak out against slavery, even at her father's parties. Her friends were shocked, but that didn't stop her.

When Elizabeth was twenty-five years old, her father died. Over the next few years, both her sister and brother got married and left home. Elizabeth wasn't ready to marry, and she decided to take a lengthy European tour. She wanted to get away and see what the world had to offer. When she returned home, Elizabeth talked her mother into freeing all their slaves. Many of them stayed on to work for the family because they had never been mistreated.

The disagreements over slavery tore the United States apart. Several Southern states left the Union. Elizabeth wasn't the only Virginian who wanted to stay in the Union. She attended the debates in the legislature. Tempers were hot and those in favor of secession from the Union threatened to harm those who opposed it.

Finally the legislature decided. Elizabeth watched in horror as the Confederate flag flew over Richmond. Even if Virginia was now part of the Confederacy, Elizabeth was determined to stick to her beliefs. Alone in her garden she made her life-changing decision: She would continue to speak out against slavery; she would be loyal to the Union, not the Confederacy.

One hundred years earlier, Elizabeth's great-aunt Letitia had aided colonists imprisoned by the British during the American Revolution. Inspired by the family stories of Letitia's daring, Elizabeth decided to help Union soldiers imprisoned in an old warehouse near her home.

In many people's opinion, Elizabeth was helping the enemy. Friends stopped calling on her and her mother—they were outsiders now and considered Union sympathizers.

Elizabeth started spying on her own. As she visited the Union prisoners, they told her about battles and troop strength. Young men from all over the South poured into Richmond, which had become the Confederate capitol, to join the Confederate army. The Union prisoners paid attention to all this. They only knew bits and pieces, but Elizabeth was sharp. She began to see the big picture of the war.

At first Elizabeth wrote letters containing the strategic information and mailed them to Union officials. Then she wrote to one of the generals and offered to spy for him. He was impressed with her understanding of war maneuvers, and he accepted. Just one thing: he wanted her to send messages in secret, not through the mail.

The Van Lews owned a farm that was just outside Richmond, so the people who worked for Elizabeth had passes to go in and out of the city. They carried many messages in hollowed-out eggs. There were other Union spies in Richmond, but Elizabeth's spy ring did the best job getting information out.

Sometimes at night Elizabeth delivered messages to a Union spy who had snuck into the city past the Confederate guards. To disguise herself, she dressed in the stained work clothes of a poor farmhand, stuffed her cheeks with cotton, and wore an old sunbonnet. No one recognized her as she rode her horse through the dark streets to her secret meeting.

Eventually it dawned on the prison guards that Elizabeth spent a lot of time talking to the prisoners. They wanted her visits to stop. That's when Elizabeth adopted her best cover. She went about town with her hair all mussed up, her clothing mismatched, talking, humming, and laughing to herself. The guards decided she couldn't really have a serious thought in her head. People who used to respect her called Elizabeth "Crazy Bet" as she passed by.

Whenever Union prisoners escaped, they knew to head for the Van Lew home, where Elizabeth would hide them in a secret room under the eaves.

Her neighbors spied on her and reported her to
the Confederate officials. Elizabeth's home was
searched and she was often followed. More
than once, Confederate detectives tried to
trick her into revealing that she was a spy
for the Union. But she seemed to have a
sixth sense about it. She never got caught.

Elizabeth grew frightened as she read
about Union spies being captured and
hung. She didn't lose her courage though.
Her work was too important. When the
Union General Ulysses S. Grant set up
camp outside Richmond, messages from
Elizabeth's spy ring flew back and forth. When
he wanted to know about the strength and location of the Confederate defenses, he sent messages to
her. He knew he could count on Elizabeth to find out.

Spy Trivia

Cryptogram: Something
written in code or cipher.
Cryptograph: A device
for writing or solving
cryptograms.
Cryptography: The art
of writing or deci-
phering messages
in code.

Finally General Grant's troops were able to break through the
Confederate defenses. Confederate President Jefferson Davis announced
that the army would leave Richmond. Many people from the city crowded
onto trains and buggies, trying to flee. But not Elizabeth Van Lew.
Overjoyed, she raised a smuggled-in Union flag of stars and stripes over her
home.

Elizabeth spent much of the family fortune helping prisoners, bribing
guards, and taking care of her spies and household workers. After the war,
she gave the rest of it to organizations to aid and educate former slaves.
When General Grant became president, he honored Elizabeth by appoint-
ing her postmaster of Richmond. But the people of the South never forgave
her. Her former friends and neighbors simply ignored her. They talked to
each other but not to her. She said it felt like when she was traveling in
Europe and couldn't understand the foreign languages.

Elizabeth was not reappointed as postmaster after President Grant was
voted out of office. She became impoverished and wrote to some of the

families of veterans she had helped when they were prisoners during the war. The families collected money and sent it to her. They were so grateful for what she had done for them.

At the end of her life, Elizabeth was lonely, but she said she would have done it all again. She didn't understand why people couldn't forgive her. She wrote in her journal that she was called names for being loyal to her country.

"Here [in the South] I am called 'Traitor,' farther North a 'spy'— instead of the honored name of 'Faithful.'"[2]

Spy Secrets:
"Crazy Bet's" Not-So-Crazy Cipher

The cipher Elizabeth Van Lew (a.k.a. "Crazy Bet") used substituted two numbers for each letter in the message. Only people who had the key to the cipher could read it. Elizabeth kept this cipher key folded in her watchcase.

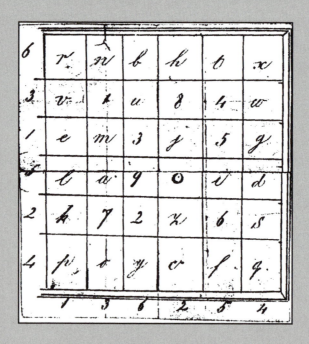

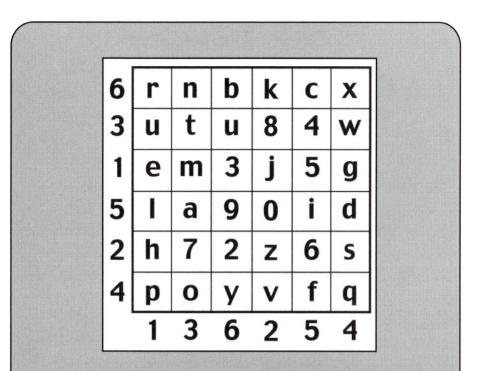

Can you decipher this message?

14434354124366

(Hint: Be sure to separate the numbers into pairs first, starting with 14.)

14 43 43 54 12 43 66

Here's How It Works

To find the letter that 14 represents, locate the number 1 in the column at the left of the grid. Then locate the number 4 in the row at the bottom of the grid. Now with your eyes or fingers, trace across the row the number 1 is in, and trace up the column the number 4 is in. The letter in that box is "g". Using this grid, you can write a message of your own.

MARY BOWSER

From Slave to Spy

c. 1839 – ?

*A*s the Davis children entered the dining room for dessert, smiles and gentle laughter replaced the adults' frowns and talk of war. The new servant, Mary, took the opportunity to glance at a paper one of the officers had carelessly placed on the side table. There were notes from the latest battle. As she scanned the page, she memorized every word. She had been listening to the war talk as she served the platters of Virginia ham, roast turkey, and oysters.

Suddenly Mary got that prickly feeling you get when you know someone is staring at you. She turned and saw Mrs. Davis frowning at her. Mary calmly but quickly picked up the bowls of pudding, bowed slightly to the Confederate First Lady, and served dessert to the eager children.

Her heart skipped a beat as it always did when she sensed the danger of being caught. Still, her disguise was perfect. No one would expect a former slave to be able to read, let alone understand anything about troop strength and war strategy.

* * * *

Mary Bowser was a former slave, but she was not uneducated. Born in 1839, she grew up in the Van Lew household. When Elizabeth Van Lew returned home from school in Philadelphia, there were lively discussions about slavery. Elizabeth spoke out against it. Mrs. Van Lew quietly agreed with her daughter. Unfortunately, Mr. Van Lew didn't agree, but he treated Mary and his other slaves with respect.

After Mr. Van Lew died, Elizabeth freed all their slaves. Then she asked Mary the most startling question: Now that Mary was free, would she like to go to Philadelphia to attend school as Elizabeth had done? Though Mary could not got to the same school as Elizabeth, she was able to attend a Quaker school for black students. Philadelphia had a strong antislavery spirit.

Many of the other freed slaves decided to stay on and work for Elizabeth. Mary may have hesitated to leave her friends and relatives, but once she got to school, her quick mind absorbed all the Quakers could teach her. She had a photographic memory, which not only helped with her studies but eventually made her a great spy.

When Confederate President Jefferson Davis moved to Richmond, he and his wife took a few of their slaves with them. They needed additional help in the Confederate White House as they had young children and all kinds of social and political obligations.

Elizabeth heard Mrs. Davis wanted more household workers, so she offered to find someone for her. Then she hurriedly sent word to Mary in Philadelphia: Would Mary come back to Richmond and take the position—as an undercover spy?

Mary agreed to return. Working in the Confederate White House she was in a great position to get secret military plans. When the baker, another Union spy, made his deliveries, Mary passed the information to him. He was amazed by her memory. Mary also met with Elizabeth. She'd set out, walking quickly, glancing over her shoulder to see who might be following her. They had hurried conversations. It must have been a relief to Mary to hear how the war was going from the Union's point of view.

When two of the Davis family slaves ran away, Mary was glad that they would find freedom. She knew what it was to be free, but even if they had asked her to join them, she wouldn't have gone. She would stay in Richmond until the war was over, doing everything she could to bring freedom to all slaves.

Over one hundred years later, in 1995, the U.S. Army inducted Mary into the U.S. Army Military Intelligence Corps Hall of Fame for her success "in a highly dangerous mission. She was one of the highest placed and most productive espionage agents of the Civil War."[1]

BELLE BOYD

"La Belle Rebelle"

1843 – 1900

Skirts flying, sunbonnet tied tightly to her head, Belle dashed across the field. All around, bullets whizzed, some ripping through her skirts. The smell of gunpowder seared her nose and eyes. The crossfire between the Union and Confederate troops at Front Royal would surely hit her before she could deliver her message to General Jackson.

How had a young southern lady gotten herself in the middle of a Civil War battle?

* * * *

Born Maria Isabella Boyd, Belle lived with her parents and seven brothers and sisters in Martinsburg, Virginia (now West Virginia). Belle's father owned a general store and managed a tobacco plantation. They lived in a two-story house covered with roses and honeysuckle.

Even as a child, Belle was a rebel. She climbed trees, raced her horse through the woods, and bossed her playmates around. Once she rode her horse into the house to protest her exclusion from an adult party her parents were planning for that night.

At twelve, Belle was sent to Mt. Washington Female College in Baltimore, Maryland, where she studied French, classical literature, and music. When she graduated at seventeen, she was formally presented to

Washington DC society. Belle enjoyed the many parties and dances. She was vivacious, attractive, and a brilliant talker. She knew how to make other people feel important.

While she was in Washington, DC, the Civil War broke out, and Belle returned to Martinsburg. She was devoted to helping her people and the rebel cause. At first, she rolled bandages and helped raise money to fund the Confederate army—duties typical of girls of that time. But soon, Belle grew bored and dissatisfied with such tame work. She wanted to do more. Her chance came when a Union army occupied Martinsburg. Using her wit and natural charm, Belle cajoled military information from Union officers. What harm would it do to chat with a pretty girl? the officers thought.

Belle sent her intelligence via messengers to Confederate leaders. Sometimes she hid the messages inside a hollowed-out watch. She even organized a spy ring with her girlfriends to get information. This was the start of Belle's career as a secret agent, and she was only seventeen.

Soon Belle was appointed by the Confederate intelligence service as a courier to Generals Beauregard and Jackson. Belle hid the military nature of her missions by pretending to be a married woman or a lost girl. This let her pass easily across enemy lines. Belle learned to use a cipher and often carried coded messages on horseback, using back roads and shortcuts. Her days as a tomboy paid off! Although she was often detained or arrested, Belle was always let go with a reprimand—until the incident at Front Royal, Virginia.

Belle was visiting her aunt in Front Royal, where Union forces had taken over her aunt's house. She learned from Union soldiers about their plan to trap General Jackson. Somehow she had to get out word of the trap. But how? Taking the message herself seemed the only way. Belle survived her hair-raising dash across the field. She told one of General Jackson's staff officers all she had learned about the strength and location of Union troops in the area of Front Royal. Jackson saved the bridges, which the Union had planned to blow up, and swept northward, nearly to Washington, DC. Belle received a thank you note from the general himself.

I thank you, for myself and for the Army, for the
immense service that you have rendered your
country today.
            Hastily, I am your friend,
            T.J. Jackson, C.S.A.[1]

Already famous in the South, the Front Royal incident made Belle Boyd notorious throughout the northern states. She became a celebrity in Europe too, where the French called her "La Belle Rebelle." Belle now was considered dangerous and was twice imprisoned. On what would be her last mission, she was caught on a steamer bound for England. She was carrying dispatches from Jefferson Davis to win Britain's help for the Confederate forces. Belle was banished to Canada, under the threat of death should she return.

From Canada, Belle sailed on to England, where she married Sam Hardinge, a Union naval officer who had taken command of the steamer after she was caught. Sam returned to the United States, intending to change sides and join the Confederate Army, but he was caught and imprisoned, leaving Belle little money to support herself and their young daughter. Still in England, Belle sold her jewelry and wedding gifts to make ends meet. She also wrote a best-selling memoir. Sam died shortly after he got out of prison and Belle was a widow at twenty-one. Ever resourceful, Belle turned to acting.

When the Civil War ended, Belle returned to the United States and continued acting. She began to give highly praised dramatic recitals of her war experiences. She was so popular that she was invited to speak all around the country. In her lectures, she stressed the importance of being one, unified country. This won her support among survivors of both the Union and the Confederates. In fact, when she died, four Union veterans lowered her coffin into the grave.

PAULINE CUSHMAN

Her Best Role

1833 – 1893

The theater was packed for the performance of Seven Sisters. Word had passed through the Confederate sympathizers all afternoon—something unexpected was about to happen on stage.

Everyone in the audience leaned forward as Pauline walked out in her role as a fashionable gentleman. She lifted a wine glass as if to drink with a friend. Then, she stepped forward and surveyed the audience. Her clear voice rang out: "Here's to Jefferson Davis and the Southern Confederacy. May the South always maintain her honor and her rights!"[1]

A shocked silence greeted her, followed by a clatter of both praise and condemnation. The stage manager rushed over. Fellow actors stared in disdain. For an instant, Pauline wished she could tell them the truth. She really supported the Union, but she had made her decision and wouldn't go back on it, even when Union guards arrived to arrest her.

As expected, the stage manager sent a note to her boarding house the next morning that read, "You will be unable to continue your present role."[2] Little did he know the new role she was about to play: Union spy.

* * * *

Pauline Cushman's birth name was Harriet Wood. She was born in New Orleans, on June 10, 1833. Her father was a merchant, and the family lived in the heart of the city. Pauline loved the bustle of the wharves and the excitement of the marketplace.

After her father lost his business, they moved to Michigan. Pauline had six brothers, and she canoed, hunted, and tracked animals through the woods as well as or better than they did.

When Eastern culture spread to Michigan, Pauline heard all about the cafes and theaters of New York. That was the life for her! She went to New York and headed straight for the theater district. Her beauty was dazzling. She had no trouble getting into a variety show, and before long she was touring with the show in the Southern states.

Pauline married one of the musicians in the show's orchestra, and they had two children who died very young. Then war broke out, and her husband became a musician in the Union army. Pauline was devastated when he died from camp fever (which could have been typhus or malaria). She threw herself into her stage career and moved to Louisville, Kentucky, to take a role in *Seven Sisters*.

Then one afternoon two Confederate officers who were visiting her made a proposal: If she dared to toast the Confederacy that night, they'd give her three hundred dollars.

Pauline was surprised. She and the actors in the company were Northerners. Kentucky was part of the Union. But she knew many of the residents of Louisville sided with the Confederates; some even spied for them.

The officers persisted, and Pauline began to warm up to the idea. Maybe she could get a name for herself as a Confederate supporter. Then maybe she could spy for the Union.

Telling the officers she'd think about it, she went straight to a Union officer. He too saw the possibilities and promised to be at the theater that night. After Pauline was arrested, he helped her develop her new role as a spy.

Confederate supporters who had witnessed Pauline's performance that night welcomed her into their social lives and into their confidence. She got a lot of information that way. Using her acting skills, she also disguised her-

self as a backwards country boy or a young gentleman to eavesdrop on conversations at the billiard parlors and other places where women weren't
allowed. In daring night rides into the countryside, she scouted out the
whereabouts of Confederate troops. Her younger days of sneaking quietly
through the woods with her playmates had given her the ability to move
unnoticed through the woodlands surrounding Louisville.

Then came a new opportunity. Pauline was invited to join the New
Nashville Theatre. She met with the head of the Union's secret operations
in the area. He didn't want to waste this spy on the stage in Nashville. He
wanted her to go right into the enemy camps to discover their strengths and
weaknesses. He hoped she could meet the famous Confederate General
Bragg and find out his plans.

One of Pauline's brothers was an officer in the Confederate army.
Though an argument had driven them apart and she hadn't seen him for
years, it would be a perfect cover: a young lady searching for her brother.
She was warned not to take notes but to keep everything in her head. If she
were caught, she could be tried—and hanged—as a spy.

The thought startled her, but Pauline wasn't about to give up. She soon
found someone willing to smuggle her across enemy lines. She met up with
a Confederate captain, who was so enamored with her he wanted her to
join his troops as his assistant. He had a Confederate uniform made for her.
Pauline played along so he wouldn't be suspicious. Lying, she promised
she'd return to serve with him after she found her brother.

At the next camp she made a big mistake. Pauline had stolen papers
from a Confederate officer and hid them—of all places—in her shoe.
When she finally met up with General Bragg, his detectives found those
hidden papers. She tried to act her way out of it. She pouted. She
wheedled. She told him she was just a Southern lady who was desperately
trying to find her brother.

Listening to her General Bragg almost felt he could believe her, but the
evidence was just too great: the papers in her shoe, the Confederate uniform—a perfect disguise for a Northern spy. General Bragg also questioned
why she hadn't smuggled in medicine, quinine to prevent malaria, and food

from the North, as other Southern ladies were doing.

The general locked Pauline in a room at a nearby inn to await trial. During her trial, Pauline made friends with one of the guards. He gave her the verdict: She had been found guilty and would be hanged. By this time, Pauline was sick from worry and a feeling of abandonment. Still she didn't have any regret. She did not renounce her country, nor did she betray her mission.

Just when she thought it was all over for her, Pauline was saved. The Union army broke through the enemy lines, forcing General Bragg and his troops to retreat. They left Pauline behind.

What a hero's welcome she received! Even the *New York Times* commended her: "Few have suffered more or rendered more to the Federal [Union] cause than . . . Pauline Cushman."[3]

But she could spy no more—everyone throughout the country recognized her face and knew that she had been a Union spy. Pauline made use of her Confederate uniform, wearing it in a one-woman show she developed about her daring adventures. She performed in Boston and other northern cities even before the war ended. After the war, Pauline toured in San Francisco and other western towns.

As the years passed, interest in the war and in Pauline's exploits faded. She remarried when her second husband died. Then she was estranged from her third husband. Her fortune faded too. Perhaps nightmares from the close calls she had haunted her. Illness led her to drug addiction. But when she died in San Francisco, the Civil War veterans had not forgotten what she had done for the Union. They gave a rifle salute during her funeral, and all those in attendance covered her grave with thousands of white flowers.

SARAH EMMA EDMONDS

a.k.a. Frank Thompson

1841 – 1898

Frank felt nervous about being interviewed by three generals, but not about the questions they would ask or the tests he'd have to take. Frank was worried that he'd be found out.

The generals fired questions at him about his loyalty, political views, and willingness to do such dangerous work. They tested his ability to handle firearms. They even did a phrenological exam, in which they examined the shape of his skull. (At that time, the form of your skull was thought to be an indication of your character and abilities.) When the generals were done, they agreed that Frank Thompson had all of the qualifications to succeed as an undercover agent for the Union's Secret Service.

Except Frank Thompson was really Sarah Emma Edmonds.

* * * *

Born in New Brunswick, Canada, Emma lived on a farm where she and her sisters and brother worked hard. Her father was mean-spirited and very strict. Their brother was often sick, so many of the farm chores fell to Emma and her sisters. They dug and sacked potatoes, chopped wood, and tended to the animals. Emma practically lived in pants and heavy shoes. She was strong and lean.

Perhaps because of her harsh life, Emma grew up with an independent spirit and a vivid imagination. Her mother worried about the risks Emma took. Emma rode the wildest horse, hunted with her father's shotgun, and climbed anything taller than she was. When Emma was twelve, a peddler gave her a novel—the first she'd ever read. It was called *Fanny Campbell, the Female Pirate Captain: A Tale of the Revolution.* The book told of a British girl who disguised herself as a sailor to rescue her sweetheart from pirates. In the book, Fanny rode tough horses, shot panthers, and even cut off her hair for her sailor disguise. It's no surprise that Emma loved reading about Fanny.

When Emma got older, her father ordered her to marry a man she didn't even know. Emma knew she had to leave. She fled to a nearby city where she learned to make and sell hats. Emma was only seventeen when she opened her own shop.

But it wasn't far enough away from her domineering father, who still wanted her to come home. Perhaps inspired by Fanny, Emma decided to dress as a man in order to start a new life. She lopped off her hair and put on men's clothing. She chose a new name: Frank Thompson. Emma found a job selling Bibles, first in Canada, then in the United States. When the Civil War broke out, she was living in Flint, Michigan.

Personal freedom was very important to Emma. She was against slavery, and though Canadian, she felt deeply loyal to the Union cause. When the Union recruiters came through Flint, Emma decided to join. The medical exam to get into the Army was simple back then—just a quick check of the legs and arms to make sure they worked okay—but Emma failed because she wasn't tall enough. The recruits marched off without her. Later, a Union officer returned to find more recruits. This time, they weren't so picky.

Farm life had made Emma strong, and she did as well as the men in basic training. Unlike the city recruits, she felt right at home handling firearms. She was ready to fight alongside the men.

With her regiment, the Second Michigan Infantry, Emma set up camp in Washington, DC, in June 1861. Like the other soldiers, she fired weapons, drilled, stood guard, and marched. For a farm girl, eating the camp hardtack and chewy rabbit soup was no problem at all.

In addition to her army duties, Emma volunteered to help in the brigade hospital. It didn't take long for her talents as a nurse to be noticed and put to use. Men got sick and died from diseases like typhoid fever and dysentery without ever reaching a battlefield.

That July, the Union's loss at the first battle of Bull Run left their troops in a state of shock. So the army was reorganized, and Emma became a mail carrier for her regiment's camp in Virginia. Then she was recommended for something a little more exciting than carrying the mail. That's when she was called to Washington, DC, and questioned by the generals.

Emma made it through the interview without her true identity being discovered. Now she had a chance to serve the Union cause as a secret agent.

Her first mission as a spy was to penetrate the Confederate lines at Yorktown, Virginia, and find out what the layout was and how much ammunition they had. How could she sneak in undetected? Emma shaved her head, put on a wig of curly hair, and colored her skin black. Disguised as a slave, she slipped into the Confederate camp where she and the other slaves built fortifications and carried water to the troops. As she passed out water, she lingered among the troops and learned how many reinforcements had arrived. She also sketched the fortification, including where guns were mounted and what kinds they were. She hid the information under the insole of one of her shoes. When she carried water to soldiers guarding the outer lines, she looked for opportunities to slip away to her own camp.

Emma penetrated enemy lines many times in various disguises. On one mission, she was an old Irish peddler. On another, a Confederate guard. Each time she was able to infiltrate enemy lines, obtain important information, and slip back to Union camps. Because of her expert riding skills and courage, she was also in constant demand as a courier, carrying messages in the midst of gunfire.

In the spring of 1863, Emma came down with malaria, and, afraid of being exposed as a woman if placed in a hospital, she deserted her regiment.

She made her way to Ohio, where she recuperated. She began wearing women's clothes again and wrote a book about her war experiences titled *Nurse and Spy in the Union Army: Comprising the Adventures and Experiences of a Woman in Hospitals, Camps, and Battlefields*. It was an instant best-seller.

Still dedicated to the Union cause, Emma returned to nursing, serving in Union hospitals until the close of the war. At Harper's Ferry, West Virginia, she met Linus H. Seelye, a carpenter. They married and had three children, all of whom died young, but they later adopted two sons who survived. Emma and Linus moved frequently, spending much of their time working in orphanages and helping former slaves find jobs and an education.

Emma wanted to apply to the government for a veteran's pension, but she knew she'd need help. No one would give a deserter a pension. She called on her former comrades to testify to her loyalty and worth as a soldier. But first she had to tell the truth. She attended a reunion of her regiment, and there she revealed herself to the men with whom she had served. Instead of being angry at her deceit, they welcomed her as one of their own and, seeing that she was in poor health, gave her their support so that she could gain her pension. It worked, and in July 1884 a special act of Congress acknowledged Emma's service as "Franklin Thompson" and placed her on the pension roll. They also deleted the charge of desertion from her record.

Emma lived the rest of her life in Texas. In Houston she was accepted into the Grand Army of the Republic, the premier organization of Civil War veterans. She was the only woman ever to receive this honor. Emma died at the age of fifty-seven and was buried with full military honors. Emma wrote in her memoirs, "I am naturally fond of adventure, a little ambitious, and a good deal romantic—but patriotism was the true secret of my success."

Spy Secrets:
Change Your Appearance

With a few tricks of the trade you can change your appearance the way secret agents do.

* Gather together: makeup that doesn't match your skin tone, and glasses, wigs, and hats from a thrift store.

* Pad your shoulders with a rolled up towel.

* Stuff a wad of gum in each cheek.

* Stick a pebble in one shoe to make yourself limp.

Experiment with different looks. Try to be older, younger, taller, or the opposite sex. Call a friend and set up a meeting spot. See if she calls your name as you walk past. No? Success!

World War I

World War I was waged between two European powers—the Central Powers of Germany, Austria-Hungary, and Turkey—and the Allies of France, Britain, and Russia, and later, the United States.

Many of these countries had espionage organizations that aimed to uncover vital secrets from their enemies. New technology for spying was now available. Aerial reconnaissance was done with airplanes instead of balloons. Sending coded signals by telegraph and radio became another important tool, and along with it, cryptography, the science of breaking those coded messages.

The United States didn't enter the war until 1917. Women replaced men in offices, and factories at home, and it was the first time American women were recruited into military service. They worked as nurses, and physical and occupational therapists, as well as operators in the Signal Corps.

While the United States sent troops to help the Allies, their involvement in intelligence gathering was small and focused on the home front. The Military Intelligence Division (MID) was a counter intelligence organization formed by the U.S. government to deal with Germany's intentions to disrupt war efforts in America.

World War I was a turning point for female spies. Although very few American women were involved in espionage, thousands of women from Britain and Europe spied for both sides. Spying had become extremely dangerous. The chivalry shown to women in previous wars was no longer apparent. Women spies who were caught were usually imprisoned or executed.

The war ended in November 1918, when German ruler Kaiser William II signed an armistice between Germany and the Allies. In January 1919 the Allies met at the Paris Peace Conference, which formally ended the war.

LOUISE DE BETTIGNIES

Spymaster

1880 – 1917

The German police matron told Louise to take off her clothing. The gruff woman rubbed Louise's skin with chemicals, trying to develop a message that may have been written on her skin in invisible ink. Under Louise's tongue, written on a pellet of rice paper, was a report of German activities. The matron was very thorough, and Louise knew she'd eventually find the pellet. Louise quickly gulped it down, but not before the matron saw her swallow.

"What did you swallow?" the woman asked Louise.

"It was nothing," Louise replied. "I'm just tired and a little nervous."

But the matron didn't believe Louise and gave her a glass of milk, to calm her nerves, she explained. Louise knew the milk contained something that would make her vomit the message, so she pretended to choke. She dropped the glass, which shattered on the floor. The matron was furious but knew it was too late for another glass—the rice paper was already being digested.

Once again, Louise had narrowly escaped the German Secret Service.

* * * *

Louise Marie Henriette de Bettignies was born in 1880 in Lille, Belgium, the daughter of a wealthy porcelain manufacturer. She was the seventh of eight children, and her upbringing was typical of many upper-class families at that time—quiet, refined, and uneventful. But Louise was not content to live a dull life. Early on, she showed signs of being exceptionally bright and insisted on going to Oxford University in England. Louise studied English, Latin, and literature. She could speak several languages.

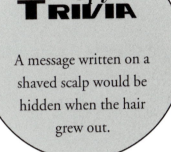

Spy Trivia

A message written on a shaved scalp would be hidden when the hair grew out.

In the early 1900s, there were few opportunities for young women with a college education, so Louise spent the next ten years as a governess for wealthy families in Austria and Italy. She was a perfect governess—educated, fun, and athletic.

By her early thirties, Louise had tired of her worldly lifestyle and wanted to help people by becoming a Red Cross nurse. When World War I broke out, the Germans swept into Belgium and occupied Lille. Before long, the beautiful city was in shambles. Hospitals and homes were filled with sick and maimed soldiers. Louise was horrified at the brutality of the war and knew she had to take a more active role in stopping it. So she exchanged her Red Cross uniform for plain clothes and began to wander the countryside, memorizing anything about the German's invasion that might help the Allied Forces.

To get her information to the Allies, Louise boarded a ferry for England, posing as a refugee. She astounded British intelligence with all she had discovered and was immediately recruited into the British Secret Service. There Louise learned about secret inks, codes, and unusual hiding places for messages. Under the secret identity of Alice Dubois, a lace maker, Louise returned to Belgium to organize a network of spies in the areas that were occupied by the Germans.

Louise immediately gathered together a special group of people. It included Dr. de Geyter, a chemist who mixed secret inks and forged identity cards, and Paul Bernard, a mapmaker, who could write 1,600 words in a space the size of a postage stamp. An old friend, Marie Leonie van Houtte, became Louise's chief assistant. With these few people, the Alice Service was born. Louise's spy network eventually grew to twelve people, then to over twenty. The members rescued and smuggled Allied prisoners of war out of German-occupied territory. They continuously passed military intelligence of vital importance to Louise. No other network in France or Belgium produced such high-quality information.

Louise sent messages in ingenious ways. She devised a code of signals using bells. She also converted balls of wool, toys, bars of chocolate, and artificial limbs into hiding places for coded messages. Once she sent the British Secret Service a tiny map, hidden in the frame of a pair of eyeglasses, that detailed the location of fourteen German ammunition dumps. On another occasion, she handed a German sergeant her latest identity card so he could stamp the photo. Little did he know that the shiny surface was a layer of thin transparent paper on which Paul Bernard had written a 3,000-word report in secret ink. One creepy, but effective, way of transporting plans and blueprints was in a coffin. The papers were tightly rolled into a glass tube and inserted into the corpse's windpipe.

One of Louise's best agents was Madame Elsie-Julie Leveugle, who lived in a chateau that overlooked Lille's railroad yards. All day and into the night, Madame would sit by a second-floor window and knit, counting the German railroad cars and troop carriers that rolled by. For each car that passed, Madame Leveugle would tap her foot on the floor. Her son, sitting in the room below, would keep count of the taps and take the tally to Louise.

German counterintelligence knew a major spy ring was operating among them and relentlessly searched for the members. But for more than

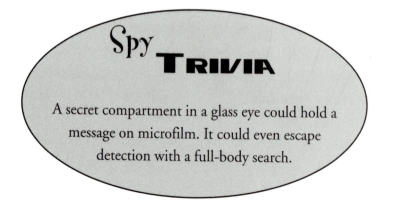

Spy Trivia

A secret compartment in a glass eye could hold a message on microfilm. It could even escape detection with a full-body search.

a year, Louise and her agents worked undetected.

Eventually, Louise and Marie Leonie were caught. They were tried by a German military court and sentenced to death. On the day they were to die, their sentences were commuted to twenty-seven years for Louise and fifteen for Marie Leonie.

Because of poor living conditions in prison, Louise grew very sick. Sadly, only forty-five days before the end of the war would have freed her, Louise died in prison.

After her death, Louise was awarded the *Croix de Guerre* and the *Ordre de L'Armes* for her bravery and service to the Allied forces. In November 1927 a statue of Louise was erected in a small square in Lille, Belgium. Her mother and Marie Leonie were honored guests.

SPY SECRETS:
Invisible Ink

For hundreds of years, invisible ink has been an important part of a spy's toolbox. Spies often wrote their secret messages between the lines of a letter. Using this recipe, write a secret message to a friend.

You'll Need

1 tsp. baking soda
1 tsp. water
small cups
toothpicks or cotton swabs
white paper
purple grape juice
paintbrush

Follow these Steps

Mix the baking soda and water in a small cup. Dip a toothpick or cotton swab into the solution and write a message on white paper. You may need to dip the toothpick often (after writing one or two letters). Let your message dry completely (at least 45 minutes). You can use a blow-dryer to shorten the drying time. Gently wipe off any excess baking soda.

Have a friend paint lightly over the area of your message with the grape juice. Voila! Your message will be revealed.

MARTHE RICHER

Double Agent

1889 – 1982

Oil sprayed Marthe's goggles. The flimsy biplane lurched and dipped, but Marthe was determined to land. She banked to the left, into the wind, and headed toward the field.

The ground came up fast. Fifty feet. Twenty feet. Down she went, pulling back on the yoke to hold the aircraft up as long as possible. The wheels thumped the ground, and Marthe's plane rolled to a stop. She climbed out and bowed elegantly to her audience as they clapped and shouted, "Tres bonne, Marthe! Tres bonne!"

At the time of this flight, Marthe Betenfeld was barely out of her teens. Soon the daring and determination she showed flying would be put to the test while spying for her country.

* * * *

Marthe was born in the eastern part of France in 1889. As a child, her sense of adventure didn't stop her from studying hard. She was especially good at languages. Besides her native French, she knew English, German, and Spanish.

After her schooling, Marthe became a dressmaker and opened her own chic shop in Paris. Her feathered hats and lace parasols were a favorite with the French ladies. Marthe also continued to fly and became one of the first female pilots in France. Her nickname was *"l'Alouette,"* which means "the lark" in French.

In 1914, the year World War I began, Marthe married Henri Richer, a lawyer who had become a pilot for the French military. Just a year later, Henri was killed in action. Marthe was devastated.

Hidden cameras were used as early as the 1880s, when they were disguised in hats.

Through Henri, Marthe had met Captain Ladoux of the French Counterintelligence Service's Fifth Bureau. Ladoux saw in Marthe the makings of a good spy. She was attractive, cultured, fluent in several languages, and anxious to revenge her husband's death. Marthe was a willing recruit.

In just a few weeks, Marthe was ready for her first assignment. Posing as a fun-loving Parisian tired of the war, Marthe traveled to Spain to penetrate the German Secret Service. In San Sebastian, the playground of Spain at the time, she took on the role of just another wealthy, glamorous woman looking for a good time. She became well known in the German social circles and quickly caught the attention of Baron Hans von Krohn, a captain in the German Imperial Navy and the Naval Attache to the Embassy at Madrid. Von Krohn was old enough to be Marthe's father, but he was smitten. When he learned of her cynical attitude toward the war, he knew he could make her a German spy—and, perhaps, his mistress.

Marthe was well aware that as a spy she might have to make difficult and dangerous choices to get the results she needed. If she became close to von Krohn, she would be privy to valuable information. She would also be putting her life on the line. But Marthe was passionate about helping the French cause. She agreed to be his mistress.

The Germans desperately needed agents in France, and Marthe was quickly put on the payroll of the German Secret Service. Her life as a double agent began.

On one of her first missions, Marthe was sent back to France to find out how many weapons and what types were being produced at a large factory outside of Paris. She left armed with the latest in invisible inks, contained in tiny tablets hidden in her fingernails. She was to use the ink to write her accounts for the German Secret Service. In Paris she made a full report to the Fifth Bureau, which was fascinated with the ink tablets. They had been able to intercept many messages in the secret writing but unable to develop them. Now that they had the tablets, their chemists could figure out exactly what chemicals were used.

A couple of weeks later, Marthe returned to von Krohn full of "secret" information concocted for her by the experts of the Fifth Bureau. Von Krohn and his chiefs in Berlin were more than satisfied. Von Krohn then sent Marthe to South America with highly secret instructions and supplies to German agents in Brazil and Argentina. These instructions were written in invisible ink on what appeared to be unused notepaper. Marthe was able to help the Fifth Bureau place one of their experts on board the ship. During the voyage to Buenos Aires, he read the instructions at his leisure.

On another mission, Marthe discovered the secret route through the Pyrenees Mountains used by German agents who infiltrated into France.

Although the Germans paid her for spying for them, Marthe never touched the money. She gave it all to France.

Baron von Krohn had fallen in love with Marthe, but for her, the arrangement was business, and her business was to get intelligence for the

Spy Trivia

Moles are enemy agents who penetrate the security services of another agency. They make their way deep into the organization and work invisibly.

French. Von Krohn took her more and more into his confidence, and Marthe's information, often written in the German's own secret ink, poured into France.

At the end of the war, Marthe returned to France. The Fifth Bureau wanted to honor her service to France, but this suggestion was turned down by authorities who could not stomach the fact that she had been von Krohn's mistress. Marthe was disgusted at their hypocritical attitude and left for England, where she married Thomas Crompton, director of the Rockefeller Foundation. No matter what the French

Spy Trivia

Double agents don't serve both sides. They deceive one side into believing they are working for it when they are actually stealing its secrets. Marthe Richer was a successful double agent.

thought, she knew in her own mind that she had served her country faithfully and well. She had done what she thought was best, and the information she had gathered was used to save countless lives. The French government finally agreed and in 1933 they made her an officer of the Legion of Honor, an honor that Napoleon Bonaparte had established to recognize distinguished service to France.

After Thomas died, Marthe returned to France. During World War II, she came out of retirement. Though well into her fifties, she worked with the French Resistance to thwart the Germans once again.

Marthe died in Paris at age ninety-two.

Spy Profile:
Mata Hari

Mata Hari was the stage name for Margaretha Geertruida Zelle, born in Holland in 1876. She was an imaginative child who was always pretending. On her sixth birthday, her father gave her a child-sized carriage pulled by two tall goats. Who knows who she pretended to be when she drove through the cobblestone streets with her school friends?

When she grew up and became an entertainer, she told people she was a temple dancer in India when she was a little girl. Almost overnight, Mata Hari became a star. She danced throughout Europe, and was in Berlin when the Germans entered World War I.

But Mata Hari's pretending got her in trouble. She lived in Paris during the war and was asked to spy for France. They told her it would be dangerous, and she got carried away with the idea. She said she wanted one big job and she wanted to be paid one million francs.

Then Mata Hari went to Spain to meet up with a German diplomat. She spent three afternoons coaxing information from him. She told him some gossip about French troops to show him she was on the German side. But he caught on to her "spying" and told her things that simply weren't true. He also sent his spies a message that he knew the French would intercept, saying Mata Hari was spying for the Germans.

Mata Hari took her information and went back to Paris. Instead of being paid, she was arrested, tried, and executed. Despite her muddled attempt to be a spy, she faced the firing squad with courage.

MARGUERITE HARRISON

Nerves of Steel

1879 – 1967

Berlin was still in a state of war, but Marguerite didn't think she'd have any problems reaching her hotel. She got in the cab and waved her travel permit at the driver, who reluctantly started off. As they neared the street where the Hotel Bristol stood, they heard gunfire. Bullets bounced off the pavement around the car. They ricocheted off buildings.

"We'd better turn back," said the driver. "No, continue on," replied Marguerite sternly. But she wondered if she'd make it through the next few blocks.

* * * *

Marguerite Elton Baker was born in October 1879 to wealthy parents. Her father prospered in Baltimore's shipping trade, and his business grew into the prestigious Atlantic Transport Lines.

Marguerite and her sister grew up on a beautiful estate near Baltimore. They were raised like royalty, with governesses, nurses, exquisite imported clothes, and trips to England and Europe. Their mother was constantly worried about Marguerite's health. She wouldn't let Marguerite play sports or have friends over—she thought Marguerite was too delicate. But Marguerite was far from delicate; she was a bold and young girl. She loved to read and learned languages easily.

When she was twelve, Marguerite went to live with her grandfather outside Baltimore and attended a nearby private school for girls. Her grandfather was an independent thinker. Marguerite spent a lot of time in his library, which was full of books on travel, exploration, and history. Her grandfather's views helped shape Marguerite's individualism.

Mrs. Baker planned for Marguerite to marry into a well-known, wealthy family, but Marguerite had other ideas. After just one semester at Radcliffe College in Cambridge, Massachusetts, she became engaged to the handsome, but poor, Thomas Bullitt Harrison. Her parents whisked Marguerite away to Europe to try to make her forget Thomas, but to no avail. Headstrong, determined, and in love, Marguerite married him. Nine months later, she gave birth to a baby boy, Tommy, and settled into homemaking. Marguerite and Thomas were happy for fourteen years, but then Thomas died, leaving her penniless.

To support her son, Marguerite turned her home in Baltimore into a boarding house. This still wasn't enough to make ends meet, so she found a job as an assistant society editor at the *Baltimore Sun* newspaper. When the United States entered World War I, Marguerite covered women's roles in the war effort. To get her stories, she drove a streetcar and worked as a laborer at Bethlehem Steel. Her expert language skills opened doors to interviews other reporters could not handle.

Marguerite wanted to do more than just be a reporter on the home front for the war cause. She was especially curious about what life was like in Germany, a country she had visited in peacetime with her family. Europe was one vast battlefield, with Germany in the center of it. Entering Germany was impossible. Not for Marguerite! She knew one way to get in: she'd become a spy.

She applied to the chief of the army's MID, General Marlborough Churchill. Marguerite impressed the general with her good looks, confidence, and fluency in so many languages. MID was convinced. But as she was about to leave for Europe, the war ended. Marguerite thought her career as a spy was over before it had even started; however, the MID had a new assignment for her. She was to go to Europe to report social, economic, and political matters to the United States delegation at the forthcoming peace conference. Marguerite was given a code name and cipher tables. She would travel as a newspaper correspondent on special assignment to the *Baltimore Sun* and write feature articles for the paper while collecting intelligence.

Marguerite's goal was to get to Berlin, the capital of Germany. Europe was in chaos. Roads were in ruins, and trains were packed with people trying to return to their homes. It took weeks of hitchhiking on army transports for Marguerite to reach Germany. Not all of the country was occupied by the Allies yet, and she found that fighting still raged in many areas, including the streets of Berlin around the Hotel Bristol.

With bullets still whizzing, Marguerite and the cabby pulled up in front of the hotel. Every curtain was pulled, every shutter was closed, and the heavy wrought-iron doors were bolted tight. The driver dumped her bags onto the sidewalk and took off without saying a word. She rang the bell and waited, pressed as closely as possible against the door. A night porter cracked the door open and poked his head out. When he saw Marguerite, he grabbed her bags and yanked her inside.

This was the start of Marguerite Harrison's life as a foreign correspondent and spy.

Marguerite quickly found her way around Berlin, mingling with people of high and low society, trying to make contact with every sort of political party. She could not overlook any happening, great or small, that might throw light on conditions in Germany. In the dead of night, after a theater performance or dinner party, Marguerite would write long reports. To keep her cover, she also filed stories for the *Baltimore Sun*.

Life as a spy was hard. For hours and hours Marguerite had to follow rumors and leads. She was always worried about being discovered. She had heard what happened to wartime spies like Mata Hari. There was nothing glamorous about her job!

The signing of the Versailles peace treaty in June 1919 ended the war and, with that, Marguerite's intelligence work in Berlin. Back in Baltimore, she realized that working for the *Sun* would not satisfy her appetite for being part of the international scene. So she turned her head toward Russia, which was in the middle of the Communist Revolution.

The Communists had overthrown the Russian elite. The country was in turmoil. Marguerite was curious about conditions there and proposed to MID to let her operate in Moscow as she had in Berlin.

It was very dangerous to enter Russia as a secret agent. Violence, terror, and executions were commonplace. Marguerite didn't speak Russian. She had no visa and would have to enter secretly by whatever route she could. Her assignment was brief: get into Russia, sum up conditions in Moscow and other key cities, and return in a few months.

With a companion to interpret for her, Marguerite set out for the Polish-Russian border. In the winter of 1920, she dashed across the border, first in a sleigh, then on foot. When she arrived in Moscow, she discovered that newspaper correspondents from the United States were not welcome. Officials said she could stay for only two weeks.

Instantly taken with the Russian people, Marguerite began to collect information as she had in Germany. She attended all kinds of meetings and talked with many types of people. She visited museums and absorbed all she could about Russian artists and writers. Her two-week stay turned into several months.

One night, Marguerite was stopped and arrested by a soldier. She was accused of being a spy. The Cheka, the secret police, even had a copy of one of her secret messages to MID from Germany. She had been betrayed! Marguerite was taken to the feared Lubianka prison.

At first she was alone in a dark, tiny cell. Then, after several weeks, she was taken to a small room full of other women. The women cleaned the one toilet that served 125 people. They hunted rats for food and made up entertainment to keep away madness. Despite their efforts, some women went crazy and were taken away raving.

Marguerite became ill and was finally moved to a better prison with real beds and flowers in the yard, but she was sure she'd die before she was freed. Back in Baltimore, Marguerite's friends, coworkers from the *Sun*, and the

MID worked to save her. Finally, she was released—still sick and thin, but alive.

Once home, Marguerite recuperated and devoted herself to lecturing and writing about her adventures in Moscow. But soon the luxuries she had dreamed of in prison became boring. So Marguerite headed to Japan to write a series of magazine articles about the Far East. This was the start of more adventures that took Marguerite around the world. Her travels included another harrowing stint in a Russian prison and making a landmark documentary film.

At age forty-seven Marguerite married an English actor and settled down. After his death, she returned to Baltimore to live near her son. She continued to travel and even returned to Berlin. When she was in her eighties, she passed alone through forbidden Communist East Berlin—once again showing her steely nerve and adventurous spirit.

Secret agent, foreign correspondent, adventurer, and filmmaker, the unconventional Marguerite Harrison died in 1967 at age eighty-eight.

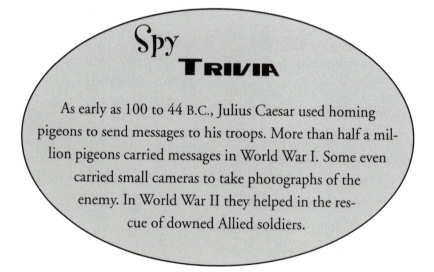

Spy Trivia

As early as 100 to 44 B.C., Julius Caesar used homing pigeons to send messages to his troops. More than half a million pigeons carried messages in World War I. Some even carried small cameras to take photographs of the enemy. In World War II they helped in the rescue of downed Allied soldiers.

World War II

World War II was fought between the Axis powers of Germany, Italy, and Japan, and the Allies: Britain, France, the Soviet Union, and the United States. By 1940 most of continental Europe was under the control of the Axis powers. Hitler planned to invade Britain next.

In 1941 the United States joined the war following Japan's attack on Pearl Harbor. U.S. troops were sent to Europe, where they fought with the Allied forces against the Germans and Italians. In Asia they battled the Japanese, who sought to expand their territory. After six years, the war finally ended in 1945.

At the start of the war the Soviet Union, Germany, Japan, and Britain had well-established foreign intelligence networks. The British Special Operations Executive (SOE) supported resistance movements, and underground organizations that used guerrilla warfare and conducted sabotage and intelligence operations in enemy-occupied territory. The United States created the Office of Strategic Services (OSS) to play a similar role. Together, and with local resistance groups, the SOE and OSS created chaos behind enemy lines in both Europe and Asia.

The Germans had two intelligence agencies, the Abwher, controlled by the Army, and the German Secret Service, run by Hitler's Nazi Party. Under the Secret Service was the Gestapo, the secret police that sought and arrested dissidents.

By World War II, women had become an integral part of the U.S. military. They served not only as nurses on nearly every front but they also ferried planes. In addition, women played important roles as spies. Many worked undercover in the resistance movements in European countries. Some spied here in the United States.

VIRGINIA HALL

Wanted! The Limping Lady

1906 – 1982

The wanted poster circulated by the Gestapo warned, "The woman who limps is one of the most valuable Allied agents in France, and we must find and destroy her." [1]

But that didn't stop Virginia Hall.

* * * *

Virginia was born in 1906 in Baltimore, Maryland, to a prominent family. She loved sports and drama. She played baseball, hockey, and tennis and acted in plays as early as the age of eight. Virginia was lucky to have a father who owned several movie theaters. She and her friends could get in for free.

In the summers, Virginia spent time on her family's farm outside of the city. There she milked cows and cared for other animals. Little did she know how valuable her farm skills would later become.

Like her grandfather, who had stowed away on a clipper ship, Virginia yearned for a life of adventure. She wanted to travel and live in faraway places. Virginia started college in the United States, but she continued her studies in Paris and Vienna, where she learned to speak French, German, and Italian. After her studies, Virginia got a job working as a clerk with the U.S. State Department in Eastern Europe. She thought a career overseas would offer her just the kind of excitement she longed for.

Then tragedy struck. While hunting in Turkey, Virginia's gun discharged by mistake and riddled her left leg with shotgun pellets. To save her life, her leg was amputated. Undaunted, Virginia learned to walk with an artificial leg, which she nicknamed "Cuthbert."

After World War II broke out, Virginia left her job. She wanted to play a more active role in fighting the Nazis. She enlisted in the French army as an ambulance driver and later joined the SOE. The commanding officers were impressed by her courage, energy, self-confidence, and cool judgement all of which were perfect qualities for a special agent. At the SOE, Virginia learned about weapons, communications, and security, all of the information she would need to become a spy.

Virginia's first assignment was to work undercover as a reporter for the *New York Post* while setting up operations in France. Working with the French underground, she helped downed American aircrews and prisoners of war to escape from enemy territory. She still found time to write for the *Post* not only to protect her cover but also to tell Americans how difficult life was for the French people as more and more Germans soldiers poured into the country, taking over homes and businesses.

Eventually it became too dangerous for Virginia, and she too had to leave France. Despite her wooden leg, she hiked in the dead of winter through the Pyrenees Mountains to get to Spain. Her wooden leg became very painful, and in a message to SOE headquarters in London, she wrote "Cuthbert is giving me trouble, but I can cope." A London agent who didn't know her replied, "If Cuthbert is giving you trouble, have him eliminated."[2] Imagine his surprise when he discovered just who Cuthbert was!

Even with the danger in France, Virginia longed for another assignment. Back in England, she trained to be a radio operator. Under the code name "Diane" she returned to occupied France, this time working with the U.S. OSS. Her mission: to maintain radio contact with London, put together sabotage plans, and form guerrilla groups to fight the Nazis.

The wanted posters were still plastered everywhere. To avoid the Gestapo, Virginia moved often and wore the long, heavy clothes of a peasant to hide her limp. For a while, she stayed on a farm in the French countryside. She milked cows and took them to pasture, noting which fields would make good spots for parachute drops. Later she moved to another house and hid her radio equipment in the attic. There she exchanged cows for a herd of goats. She'd tend the herd along the roads where she knew she could watch German troop movements. Delivering goat milk turned out to be a perfect way to make contact with the local resistance.

Despite intensive searching by the Gestapo, Virginia continued to send radio messages to London about German army activities. She also organized farmhands to receive parachute drops of weapons and supplies from England. Although her leg kept her from being trained in guerrilla warfare, Virginia became a superb leader. Her resistance teams destroyed bridges, derailed freight trains headed for Germany, downed key telephone lines, and took Nazi prisoners.

The Gestapo never found the Limping Lady.

At the war's end, Virginia received America's Distinguished Service Cross. She was the only female civilian in the war to receive this high honor. Virginia continued to use her skills and experience and became one of the first women employed by the Central Intelligence Agency (CIA), the successor organization to the OSS. She went overseas on several more assignments but spent her last years with the CIA in Washington, DC.

Reflecting on her career, Virginia said, "I look to the new achievements the next generation will accomplish as they carry the torch into the future, and I hope that they will follow my example and never let anything hold them back."[3]

Spy Profile:
Julia Child's Shark Repellent

Julia McWilliams was born in 1912 in Pasadena, California. As a child, she was fun loving and mischievous. She played tennis, wrote stories, and performed plays. She loved to take her father's cigars and smoke them in a hiding place with friends.

Julia went to Smith College in Northampton, Massachusetts, where she majored in history. Over six feet tall, Julia was a key player on the basketball team. In college, she kept everyone laughing with her great sense of humor.

When World War II broke out, Julia volunteered with the Red Cross in Pasadena, then got a clerical job in Washington, DC, with the OSS. There she helped develop a shark repellent to keep sharks from bumping into underwater explosives and setting them off. Her recipe for this repellent is still used today.

Julia then volunteered to help staff a new overseas OSS base in Ceylon (now known as Sri Lanka). Important missions against the Japanese were launched from that area, and the OSS provided the U.S. military and State Department with intelligence about the enemy. While in Ceylon, Julia met the worldly, sophisticated Paul Child, who also worked for the OSS. From Paul, she learned about the joy of good food.

They fell in love and married when they returned to the United States. Later, Paul was stationed in Paris with the U.S. State Department, and Julia went with him. While living in Paris, Julia began cooking professionally. The rest is culinary history.

GERTRUDE S. LEGENDRE

Making Her Mark

1902 – 2000

Gertrude was picked up in a small car and driven through war-torn Frankfurt to the German-Swiss border. There she boarded a train for Switzerland, shadowed by a tall stranger in a light overcoat.

Once on board, Gertrude kept out of sight, hiding behind empty seats. The train moved slowly, inching along battered tracks. It stopped just short of the gate on the German side of the border. Gertrude wasn't safe yet. She slipped off the train. What should she do next? She turned around to see the mysterious man in the light overcoat right behind her.

"Run," he whispered and gestured with his arm toward the Swiss guard post.[1]

Gertrude ran. Suddenly she heard, "Halt!" It was an armed German border guard. She'd been seen.

* * * *

Gertrude Sanford was born in Aiken, South Carolina, in 1902. She was the youngest of three children; her brother, Laddie, was oldest, then came sister Janie, and then Gertie, as she was always called.

Gertrude grew up in rural New York State, where her family made carpets and raised thoroughbred horses. When she was a teenager, her family moved to New York City. Gertrude's mother took in the lavish roaring twenties lifestyle; there were always parties, dances, musicals, and the theater to attend.

But Gertrude wanted more than a whirling social life. At the Foxcroft School in Virginia, she was greatly influenced by the headmistress, who convinced all the girls to make their own mark in life.

Hunting in the country had always been part of her early life and it became a lifelong passion. At age eighteen, instead of staying in New York for the debutante parties, Gertrude hunted in the Grand Tetons. At twenty-five, she went on her first African safari.

In London, during the summer of 1928, she met tall, handsome Sidney Legendre. Sidney accompanied Gertrude to Africa to collect specimens for the American Museum of Natural History in New York. They fell in love and married, settling down in South Carolina on a large plantation called Medway.

When World War II began, Sidney entered the Navy. Gertrude wanted to be part of the war effort too, so she volunteered with the OSS in Washington, DC. She worked her way up from file clerk to head of the cable desk, where she monitored communications from U.S. secret agents all over the world. On her desk were piles of folders stamped "Restricted," "Confidential," "Secret," and "Top Secret." It was an enormous responsibility for Gertrude to have knowledge of such vital information.

Soon Gertrude transferred to the OSS office in London as Chief of the Central Cable Desk. She handled incoming messages for thirteen OSS branches in London. The steel safes in her office were filled with secret files from North Africa, Italy, Sweden, India, China, Ceylon, and outposts in German-occupied France.

Gertrude was transferred to an OSS center in Paris. While the offices were being renovated, she obtained a five-day pass—a well-deserved chance to do what she wanted for a few days. Whether it was her sense of adventure or desire to see action after so many months behind a desk, Gertrude certainly didn't expect her next decision to be such a dangerous one.

Accompanied by OSS colleagues Bob Jennings and Major Max Papurt, Gertrude decided to see what it was like at the battlefront. With the major's driver, they set out in a jeep for Wallendorf, a small German village near the front lines. Just as they neared the signpost for Wallendorf, bullets hit the jeep. They hurled themselves to the ground. But Papurt and the driver were hit, and there was nothing to do but surrender. Jennings pulled a white handkerchief from his pocket and tied it to the end of Papurt's rifle. He hoisted it high above the jeep.

With the Germans nearly upon them, Gertrude quickly burned their passes and any other papers that would link them to the OSS. At the same time, they came up with believable cover stories.

The driver and Papurt were transferred to a medical unit, but Gertrude and Jennings were taken to a bunker and interrogated. Gertrude repeated her cover story in French: She was a clerk at the American Embassy acting as a translator for Jennings. They had been misinformed that Wallendorf was in American hands. She knew nothing of any importance. (This couldn't have been farther from the truth.)

Gertrude recited her cover story many times during the next six months. She was moved from prison to prison. At one, a huge castle, Gertrude noticed that Lt. William Gosewich, the German officer in charge, spoke fluent English, with just a trace of a New York accent. Lt. Gosewich interrogated Gertrude every evening. Over the next several weeks, his questioning became more relaxed. Gertrude learned that he had gone to school in New York City and had married an American. They had lived in the United States for eighteen years. He and his family were visiting Germany when the war broke out, and Gosewich had been forced to serve. He loved his native Germany but opposed the war.

Gertrude formed a friendship with Gosewich that probably saved her life. Gosewich was sorry Gertrude had been captured and worked to get her released. He also tried to keep the infamous Gestapo away from her.

One day Gosewich told Gertrude he had been called to the front for three weeks. While he was gone, Gertrude was taken to Gestapo headquarters in Berlin. Despite intense interrogation, Gertrude never revealed anything. Finally, she was transferred to a large estate-turned-prison, where she was able to contact Gosewich. He came to see her and planned her escape to Switzerland.

When Gertrude approached the Swiss border, she didn't stop when she heard the German border guard call "Halt!" She ran with all her might toward the Swiss gate. The guard's footsteps grew closer.

The Swiss sentry shouted, *"Identite! Identite!"* all the while raising his gate.

"American passport!" Gertrude screamed and passed under the lifted barrier.[2]

Safely in Switzerland, Gertrude was met by OSS officials with hundreds of secrets still safe. She was sent home and reunited with her husband and family. Gertrude never knew why the German guard didn't shoot her. When her husband got out of the Navy, they returned to Medway and continued their life of traveling and hunting. Gertrude was able to pay back Lt. Gosewich's kindness by helping him and his family return to the United States.

Sidney died of a heart attack in 1948, but Gertrude continued to travel, visiting exotic places such as the Galapagos Islands, New Guinea, and the Amazon. She grew concerned about the plight of endangered animals and turned her plantation into a center for saving endangered birds. At the time of her death in 2000, Medway Plantation became a wildlife preserve.

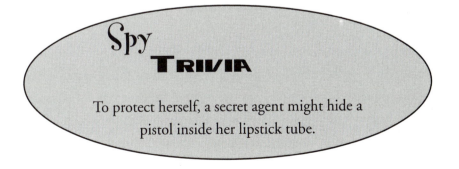

Spy TRIVIA

To protect herself, a secret agent might hide a pistol inside her lipstick tube.

MARIA GULOVICH LIU

Shadow Warrior

1921 –

The Gestapo started at each end of the train, checking everyone's luggage. The train was so packed that Maria had to stand. She clutched the suitcase she was carrying for the Slovak underground. It was locked, and she had no key. She didn't know what was inside, only that it was important. She couldn't let the Gestapo get their hands on it.

Across from her was a compartment full of German officers on their way to the front. Maria smiled at one of them. She tried to look uncomfortable wedged between the passengers. Luckily, the officer offered Maria a place to sit. He took her suitcase, and she went inside their compartment. Just then, the Gestapo passed by. They saluted the officers and kept going. If they had discovered the radio inside the suitcase, Maria would have been arrested and shot.

* * * *

Maria Gulovich was born in 1921 in the Slovak village of Jakubany, near the border with Poland. She was the oldest of six girls. Maria's father, Edmund, was a Greek Orthodox priest and her mother, Anastasia, was a teacher. Jakubany was very rustic. There was no electricity or running water. There was one telephone at the post office, and the grocery store was several miles away. Most people farmed, logged, or raised sheep for a living. Between school and chores, Maria didn't have much free time. Whenever she could, she hid in the hayloft of the barn and read books. During summer vacations, she went into the nearby hills and gathered strawberries and mushrooms. In the winter, she sewed dresses for her sisters.

Maria started school in a one-room schoolhouse, but her father worried that she wasn't getting a good education. He eventually sent Maria to two different convents in the city of Presov. It was not easy for Maria to conform to the strict convent lifestyle. She was free-spirited and had a mind of her own, but she was also a good student. She studied literature and history. She already knew how to speak Hungarian and Rusyn (a dialect of Russian), and at school she learned to speak Russian, German, and Slovak.

When Maria turned fourteen, her father sent her to Vienna to live with an aunt and begin an apprenticeship as a dressmaker. Maria loved Vienna with its rich culture and museums. There was so much to see and do. Eventually, Maria enrolled in a teacher's college. She began teaching school in a town not far from her family home in Jakubany. Maria enjoyed being a teacher, but with the arrival of the war, the job did not last long.

The new German regime, the Third Reich, occupied most of Czechoslovakia. In Slovakia, where Maria lived, the people were supposedly free, but Hitler's puppet government and local Nazis controlled almost all aspects of their lives. They hunted down anyone who didn't agree with them. Maria hated that her country was under Nazi rule.

Soon after Maria started teaching, her school was taken over by the German army. The Nazis planned to invade the Soviet Union, and the little town of Jarabina where she taught was right along the route. They wanted to use the town as a staging area for German armed forces.

In the spring of 1943, Maria moved to the farming community of Hrinova. For a while, she taught school there. Some of the Slovak people organized an underground movement to help the Allies defeat Germany and reclaim their country. Maria decided to join them.

Going undercover as an apprentice dressmaker, Maria moved to the new resistance headquarters in Banska Bystrica and carried secret messages for the Slovakian Underground. It was a dangerous job, but Maria was dedicated to freeing her people from Nazi control. Maria later worked as a translator and interpreter for the Russians in Banksa Bystrica who were organizing guerrilla groups to fight the Nazis. She translated Slovak messages from the front line into Russian.

Now that a strong resistance movement was in place in Slovakia, the OSS flew agents in to help the uprising and rescue downed U.S. airmen. Maria met some of them when they came to Banska Bystrica.

No one expected the Germans to react so strongly to the uprising. Huge numbers of troops poured into Slovakia to break up the rebellion. The airfield and Banska Bystrica were bombed every day. The OSS couldn't get all of the downed airmen out. The Slovakian Underground was collapsing.

The Germans tightened their net around Banksa Bystrica. Nearly everyone left the city, including Maria and the American agents. They headed for Donovaly, a ski resort in the Tatra foothills. But by the time they arrived, the ski resort had to be abandoned because German troops were advancing so quickly. Maria, along with downed Allied pilots, members of the British and American intelligence teams, and other refugees, pushed deeper into the frigid, unmapped trails of the Tatra mountains—the only way to the Russian front and their freedom. They had no idea what lay ahead.

They decided to split into smaller groups. Since Maria knew the area, she helped lead an OSS team of twenty men, acting as their guide and interpreter. Whenever they could, they camped in abandoned huts in the mountains and foraged for food at farms and villages. Food was so scarce that they once had to eat a dead horse to survive. They began to suffer from frostbite. Their feet swelled and turned black.

While looking for food, six people in Maria's group were captured by the Germans. She and the rest finally reached the mountain resort village of Velky Bok, where the British had set up refuge in a hotel. Maria and the OSS team spent Christmas Eve in a nearby hut, safe for a few days. On Christmas Day, Maria, two OSS agents, and two British officers headed for the hotel. While they were gone, Nazis surrounded the hut, took everyone captive, and set fire to it. Maria and her companions had barely escaped.

For twenty-three more days, they marched toward the Russian front, suffering from hunger and cold. Several times they were nearly captured. At the end of January, Maria and her tattered group huddled in an abandoned mine shaft near the village of Bystre, not far from the Hungarian border where the Russians were fighting. They lay like logs, packed tightly, head to toe. After a week, they moved to a larger mine with many other refugees. One day they heard shouting. The Germans had abandoned Bystre. Allied forces occupied the village. They were free!

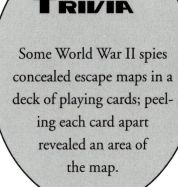

Spy Trivia

Some World War II spies concealed escape maps in a deck of playing cards; peeling each card apart revealed an area of the map.

It was five more months before Maria finally made it to OSS headquarters in Italy, where she would be truly free. General William Donovan, head of the OSS in Washington, DC, arranged for Maria to go to the United States in January 1946 as an exchange student.

On a spring day in 1946, at a ceremony at West Point, General Donovan pinned the Bronze Star onto Maria for her heroic actions. She was the first woman to be decorated at West Point in front of the Corp of Cadets. Maria was only twenty-four.

Maria settled down in the United States. She lives in California with her husband, Hans Liu.

In 1945 two of the men Maria accompanied wrote: "Her courage and abilities are admired and appreciated by all the men, especially us, whom she accompanied through the lines. She is responsible for our being alive today."[1]

JOSEPHINE BAKER

Forever Grateful

1906 – 1975

Rap-rap-rap. *The knocks were loud and insistent. Josephine hurried the other spies into a back room and opened the door. Five German officers pushed past her, demanding to search her chateau for weapons.*

Josephine took command of the situation, just as she always did on stage. Josephine was an African American and she also had some Native American ancestry. When they said "weapons," it made her think of tomahawks. She joked that there were no tomahawks in her home. "And," she added, "the only dance I've never taken part in is the war dance." [1]

The officers laughed, chatted with her for a while, then left without doing a search. Josephine and the other spies hiding in her chateau were safe for the moment.

* * * *

Josephine's given name was Freda Josephine. She was born on June 3, 1906, in St. Louis, Missouri, to Carrie MacDonald and Eddie Carson. Her mother, Carrie, had moved to St. Louis during the 1904 World's Fair, hoping to become a dancer. Carrie's career never took off, and she raised her four children in extreme poverty. One year, Josephine wore the same blue dress to school every day. Students teased her mercilessly.

When Josephine was ten years old, a medicine man came through town and set up a vaudeville show with all kinds of acts to hawk his wares. Josephine, moved by the music, danced across the stage. The audience loved her, and the medicine man gave her a dollar. It amazed her that she could earn money doing something she loved.

Several years later, Josephine joined the vaudeville circuit and traveled throughout the eastern United States. When she was only fifteen years old, she married Willie Baker and settled in Philadelphia. She kept dancing and acting in clubs and dreamed of performing in New York.

When she had enough money in her pocket, Josephine decided to leave her husband and head for New York. She joined a chorus line and soon stole the show with her comic antics as well as her amazing dancing. She was invited to perform in Paris. Josephine wasn't sure about leaving America, but she soon discovered that the Parisians loved her. And in Paris she did not experience the same racial prejudice as in the United States. Josephine became a star, performing on stages all over Europe and in South America.

When the Nazis came to power in Germany, Josephine's picture appeared on the cover of a propaganda pamphlet denouncing many famous performers who did not meet the Nazi ideals of racial purity. One terrible night in 1938, Nazis attacked Jewish homes throughout Germany and Austria. Josephine, who by then was married to a Jewish man, wanted to stand up publicly for her beliefs. She joined the International League Against Racism and Anti-Semitism and was soon recruited by the French Resistance.

Josephine was not afraid of possible consequences. "France made me what I am," she said, "I will be grateful forever . . . . [The people of Paris] have given me their hearts, and I have given them mine. I am ready . . . to give them my life."[2]

She began her undercover work at the embassy parties she was often invited to because of her stardom. Josephine listened carefully to talk about German troop strength and locations and passed it on to other Resistance agents. She was most famous for getting the original copy of the German-Italian codebook. Unbelievable as it was, an official from the Italian Embassy simply gave it to her.

During this time, Josephine also helped serve meals to refugees who flooded into Paris. As the Germans advanced into France, she visited the injured in hospitals, sometimes cheering them by singing in the wards.

Then Paris was invaded. The show Josephine was starring in closed down. From her chateau in southern France, she and other secret agents continued to work for the French Resistance. As an actress, Josephine was allowed to travel across borders to perform in other countries. Her sheet music often had top-secret information written in invisible ink between the bars of music. Eventually, she went to North Africa and performed throughout the area, raising money for the French Resistance.

After the war Josephine received many awards from the French government for her war service, including the *Croix de Guerre*. She toured the United States several times, taking opportunities to speak out for civil rights. She was on the platform in front of the Lincoln Memorial in Washington, DC, with Martin Luther King, when he gave his famous "I Have a Dream" speech.

But her home was in France. Josephine never gave up the stage. During the run of a new show to celebrate her fiftieth year of performing, she suffered a stroke and died. The people of Paris gave her their hearts once again. They lined the streets as her coffin passed to honor their star, their war hero, and their champion of freedom and equality.

Several years before her death, a committee of distinguished people proposed that Josephine win the Nobel Peace Prize. She told them she didn't deserve it. She said, "It should be shared by each man and each woman on this Earth who struggles to love and live in peace."[3]

Spy File:
Josephine's Rainbow Tribe

After the war, Josephine reflected on the horrors she had witnessed. She wondered what it would take for people to work together to prevent other wars.

An idea grew within her. She eventually adopted twelve children from differing ethnic and religious backgrounds. She raised them together, free from prejudice. She called them her Rainbow Tribe and hoped they would be ambassadors of peace in the world.

Josephine was not able to spend as much time as needed raising the children because of her touring and performing, and the members of the Rainbow Tribe were forced to go their separate ways. Still, as adults they all held her in high regard.

NOOR INAYAT KHAN

Light of Womanhood

1914 – 1944

Saturday, June 26, 1943. *"Madeleine" couldn't believe her ears. All the members on the spy team she'd just joined had been arrested—all but her. Her heart beat as fast as her fingers tapped out the transmission to London. It's too dangerous for you now,* they replied. Come back. Immediately!

But "Madeleine" knew there was no other wireless operator in Paris. How would secret messages get through without her? She decided to take her chances. She had the courage to stay right under the noses of the Gestapo.

* * * *

"Madeleine" was the code name for Noor Inayat Khan, one of the Gestapo's most sought-after British spies. Noor's given name meant "Light of Womanhood." She was born on January 1, 1914, in Moscow. Her father, Inayat Khan, had gone there to spread Sufism, an Islamic mystic philosophy that teaches acceptance of all religions.

The family fled to England when the Russian Revolution broke out. They later moved to Suresnes, a small town on the outskirts of Paris. Both Noor's parents were deeply spiritual. Her mother, Ora Ray Baker, was American born and a relative of the founder of Christian Science. Inayat Khan shared his love of music with his children. All the children grew up playing various instruments and even composing music.

Noor entered school when she was seven years old. Her family life was so intellectual and serious that she didn't know how to play with other girls. She did make a few close friends, but she was okay with being alone.

While on a trip to his homeland of India, Noor's father died, and her mother plunged into a four-year depression. Noor took over managing the household and raising the younger children, which was a big responsibility for a thirteen-year-old, but she accepted it without question. She continued going to school, and if she had any free time, she read. Joan of Arc, who fought and died for her beliefs, became her heroine.

Noor eventually graduated from the Sorbonne, a famous university in Paris. She was just beginning her career as a children's book author when the Germans invaded Paris. One afternoon, as she sat with her brother discussing what to do about the war, she heard gunfire. They had been taught to accept everyone, even people they disagreed with, but in a flash, both realized they wanted the Nazis stopped. They would do anything to help. For safety's sake, they made the decision to move to England.

Noor studied nursing with the Red Cross, but that didn't feel like enough. She entered the Women's Auxiliary Air Force and was at the top of her class for speed in sending wireless messages. She worked for a while sending and receiving messages from British bombers on their missions.

One day she was summoned by an official in the War Office and asked if she would use her skills in Paris for the SOE. The official made it clear that if she were caught by the Gestapo, she could be tortured or even executed.

Noor didn't need to think twice before saying yes. "Madeleine" became a spy.

Unfortunately, within two weeks of her arrival in Paris, her team members had all been arrested. Noor immediately searched out places where she could set up her transmitter to send and receive messages. She located safe places for parachute drops of food and cargo, arranged help for agents who needed to escape from France, and described what the Germans were planning next.

Noor transmitted messages at least four times a day, each time from a different apartment in a different part of Paris. All she needed was a room with a window next to a tree. The aerial—a thin, leaf-green rod—had to be hidden in the tree branches. If the Gestapo spotted it, they could easily find her.

Noor was always on the run because wireless operators couldn't transmit for more than thirty minutes at a time for fear the Gestapo, driving up and down the streets with detectors, would pinpoint their location. Friends who saw her wondered if she ever had time to eat or sleep. When she did have a chance to sit and talk for a few minutes, she usually dozed off.

In her search for safe houses, Noor went to Suresnes. She was always in disguise; her hair was red one day, and bleached blonde the next. She always wore dark glasses. Still, the people in her old neighborhood recognized her. Was she afraid? they asked. But she wasn't. She had a calm certainty that those who knew her would never betray her.

Other agents continued to be arrested. One day agent "X" missed a meeting with her. She telephoned him and someone with a strange voice answered. "X" came to the phone and set up another meeting. A third agent was with Noor. Suspicious, he went along to check it out. He spotted "X" on a park bench, surrounded by Nazi agents. Noor narrowly escaped capture.

When one of the apartments Noor used was searched, agent "Y" said he wouldn't continue working with her because it was too dangerous. "Y" put Noor on a train to Normandy, where he had found a safe place for Noor to hide. Two days later, he saw her back in Paris.

Noor just would not give up. If anything, she worked harder, moving relentlessly about the city searching for places to transmit her messages. Then it happened. An acquaintance of the landlady at one of Noor's apartments sold information of her whereabouts to the Gestapo. An officer was waiting inside the door one afternoon. He grabbed her and she bit him, fighting desperately. She was tiny, barely over five feet tall, but she put up a good fight. He had to call for help to take her in.

At Gestapo headquarters she asked to use the bathroom, and the next thing the officials knew she'd gone out the window and was running across the roof!

Noor was caught again and questioned daily, but she wasn't tortured. In fact, the officials came to respect her bravery and gentility. She was given pen and paper and she spent her time writing and reading; however, when she and two other prisoners were caught in another escape attempt, Noor told the official in charge she'd do anything to escape and go back to spying. He sent her to a prison in Germany, where she was put in chains.

On September 12, 1944, Noor and three other women prisoners were taken to the concentration camp at Dachau and executed. Noor was awarded the George Cross by the British and the *Croix de Guerre* by the French for her heroic service.

Noor had been engaged when she was a university student. When the war started, she broke off the engagement, wanting to be free to serve. After the war, her fiancé wrote, "She brought a new light and life. She had the best heart one could ever meet. . . . One glance of her was like a thousand suns."[1]

SPY FILE:
Noor's Jataka Tales

Noor had an active imagination. She believed she saw fairies when she was very young, and she made up stories, songs, and poems about all kinds of things. As she grew up, she got to know a children's illustrator, H. Willebeek Le Mair. Le Mair asked Noor to work on a book project retelling stories of the reincarnations of Buddha in animal form in which he taught lessons of self-sacrifice. Together, they published *Twenty Jataka Tales*.

"The Fairy and the Hare" was Noor's favorite story. In it, the hare offers to give himself to a starving old beggar so he could eat. At once, it is revealed that the starving old man is really the fairy Sakka. The fairy tells the hare, "The kindness of your heart, O blessed one, shall be known throughout the world for ages to come."[2]

Like the hare, Noor is known throughout the world for her great kindness and the courage she had in sacrificing herself to spy for freedom.

BETTY PACK

Code Name "Cynthia"

1910 - 1963

Betty knew that stealing the naval codes would be difficult, but not impossible. She was ready. Shortly after midnight, she and her friend, Charles, walked to the French Vichy Embassy, which was pro-Nazi, and opened the front door with Charles's key. They talked softly in the reception room. When a guard came to investigate, Betty quickly embraced Charles. The guard, seeing what appeared to be two lovers, muttered an apology and left.

Betty hurried to the door of the naval intelligence office and started to pick open the padlock, just as she had practiced so many times. Her hands shook as she worked the lock. Stay calm, she reminded herself, concentrate. The lock popped open. Then Betty opened a window to let in an OSS safecracker. In minutes, the safecracker had opened the door to the safe inside the intelligence office and removed the code books. He climbed back out the window, down the ladder, and into a waiting car. The car whisked him to a hotel where an OSS team was set up to photograph the codes.

Betty and Charles anxiously waited for the safecracker to return with the books. The deadline was four in the morning. By 4:30, no one had appeared. Something had gone wrong.

* * * *

Betty was born Amy Elizabeth Thorpe in November 1910 in Minneapolis, Minnesota. Her father, George, was an ambitious Marine Corp officer, and her mother, Cora, was a well-educated, worldly person interested in good manners and being active in society. Betty had a younger sister, Jane, and a brother, George.

When Betty's father retired from the military, he took his family on a grand tour of Europe. Then they settled in Washington, DC, where her father practiced maritime law. They became prominent members of Washington society.

Betty grew up to be a beautiful and slender young woman with reddish-blond hair and green eyes. She attended Wellesley College in Massachusetts, where she studied music. Betty had a mind of her own and, although she was raised to be a debutante, she thought that Washington, DC society was silly and superficial.

To the surprise of her family, at twenty-one Betty married an older man named Arthur Pack, a diplomat who worked at the British Embassy in Washington, DC. After their marriage, Arthur was transferred to the British Embassy in Chile and then to Spain.

Betty was thrilled to be in Europe, but though they had a daughter, she was often lonely and bored. While they were in Spain, a civil war broke out between the Communists and Nationalists. When the embassy moved from Madrid, Betty and her husband moved to Biarritz, just across the French border. One day, Betty met five young revolutionary soldiers. They asked Betty to help them get away from the Communist-held areas before they were caught. Betty didn't hesitate. She loaded them into her car and drove them to France, right through the enemy checkpoints. Because of her diplomatic license plate, she wasn't stopped. This adventure stirred Betty up. She wanted to do more to help the causes she believed in.

Spy Trivia

The wristwatch camera dates from 1948. The camera can take eight pictures the size of a little fingernail.

The Packs were transferred again, this time to the British Embassy in Warsaw, Poland. War in Europe was about to erupt. Hitler had already conquered Austria and was eyeing Czechoslovakia. Poland was in the middle of it all.

At embassy dinners and receptions, Betty often overheard important information. One evening she heard about Poland's secret plans to deal with Hitler. Betty told everything she had heard to a British official at the embassy. The official revealed that he was part of MI6, Britain's Secret agency abroad, and he asked Betty to get more information for him. A spy was born!

Betty's job was to do lots of entertaining, widen her circle of contacts, then charm highly-placed officials into talking too much. Betty loved the idea of being a spy and helping the Allied cause. The work was challenging, and she was no longer bored. When Arthur was reassigned to Chile, Betty decided not to go. There was little to spy on in Chile, so she returned to the United States alone.

It wasn't long before the British Intelligence contacted Betty again. She was officially recruited into their service under the code name "Cynthia," and she was to operate in the Washington, DC, area. On one mission she arranged to meet the naval diplomat of the Italian Embassy. The diplomat fell in love with Betty and, before long, gave her the Italian naval codes. The Allies read the codes, which allowed the British fleet to win a decisive victory over the Italian Navy in 1941 in the Mediterranean.

The British wanted the French Vichy naval codes next. The Allies were planning to invade Vichy territory in North Africa, so the code books might prove invaluable. It was Betty's biggest assignment yet. Could she pull it off?

At the French Vichy Embassy in Washington, DC, Betty met Charles Brousse, a French diplomat who worked there. She hoped to convince Charles to help her. Despite working with the Vichy French, Charles detested the Germans and was pro-British. Charles wanted to help Betty, but the codes were in an embassy vault that he did not have access to. They were contained in two thick dictionary-sized volumes, locked in a safe inside a padlocked room. The embassy was patrolled by an armed watchman and a vicious guard dog. In addition, the Vichy secret police might be watching. But then the American OSS offered to help, and a daring plan was hatched—a plan to steal, photograph, and return the code books, all in just a few hours.

Things went as planned until the 4 A.M. deadline was missed. Where was the safecracker?

Finally, at 4:40, he appeared, much to Betty's relief! The team at the hotel had taken longer than expected to photograph the codes. The safecracker climbed back up the ladder, returned the code books to the safe, shut everything up again, and disappeared out the window. Betty and Charles calmly left the embassy and walked to the hotel.

Several months later, the Allies launched Operation Torch, the invasion of French North Africa. The Nazis were taken completely by surprise. How had the Allied forces known so much? Six months later, all of North Africa was in Allied control, thanks in part to the courage and daring of "Cynthia."

After her success at the French Vichy Embassy, Betty retired from spying. She and Charles had fallen deeply in love. Betty divorced Arthur and married Charles. They moved to an old French chateau in the Pyrenees Mountains.

Years later, Betty grew seriously ill with cancer. Before she died, she wrote her autobiography and many articles about her life as a spy.

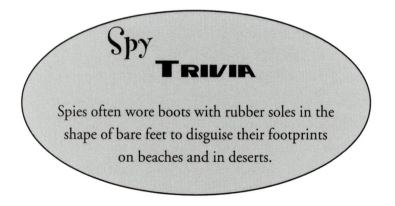

Spy Trivia

Spies often wore boots with rubber soles in the shape of bare feet to disguise their footprints on beaches and in deserts.

The Chinese Revolution

Although the United States and the Soviet Union never fought against each other, the two superpowers took sides in other countries' armed struggles all over the world. One important uprising was the Chinese Revolution. The Chinese Nationalist party, led by Chiang Kai-shek, was driven out of mainland China by the Communists to Taiwan. In 1949 China became the People's Republic of China. In Asia communism also gained footholds in Vietnam and Korea.

EVA WU

Daring Dancer

---

c. 1934 – ?

Eva *turned toward her audience to begin dancing. Her heart started to pound. The policemen who had questioned her earlier that afternoon entered the room. There too, on the other side of the room, was her contact, a Nationalist secret agent. Wound in Eva's hair was a white chrysanthemum, a signal to the agent that her latest mission had gone well.*

With the Communist police at her show, she should have been wearing a red flower to warn the agent that danger was nearby. How could she change the white flower to red?

* * * *

Eva Wu was born in China around 1934. Not much is known about her childhood, except that she was one of fifteen children. Her father was a wealthy doctor in Canton.

In 1949 the Communist party came into power. Eva's father feared that the Communists would take all of his money, so he dispersed his family, giving each member a small amount of gold—enough to get settled somewhere away from Canton.

Eva made her way to Hong Kong, which was at that time a British colony. She became a dancer at a cosmopolitan nightclub. People from all over the world came to see her dance. One of her most famous perfor-

112

mances was a temple dance to keep away evil spirits. In one hand, Eva carried a jade-handled dagger and in the other, a bowl of water. With graceful gestures, Eva gave the impression that she was purifying herself, the audience, and all of the land around them. At the end of the dance, the audience often sat silently entranced, so enchanting was Eva's beauty and the movements of her dance.

But while Eva enjoyed dancing, she wondered how she could help rid her country of the Communists. Her answer came one night in the form of a stranger who met with her after the show. He asked if she would like to serve her country.

Eva agreed to help the stranger, who was really a secret agent for the Nationalist Party. He explained to Eva that her missions would be simple: she would serve as a courier, smuggling messages out of Hong Kong into nearby Kowloon, a Communist-held city. She already had the perfect disguise—a dancer browsing the shops in Kowloon for silks, brocades, and perfumes. To find out how her mission went, the intelligence officer would attend her shows. If all had gone well, Eva would wear a white chrysanthemum in her hair. If she needed to warn him, the flower would be red.

On Eva's first mission, she had a written message hidden in her mass of shiny black hair, which she arranged in loops. During an "innocent" shopping expedition in Kowloon, Eva easily passed the letter to a shopkeeper, another Nationalist agent.

On later missions, Eva's reports were hidden on microfilm. Anyone watching this fragile-looking dancer finger a swatch of silk or buy a new costume would never have suspected her of transferring spy documents. Yet Eva became an important undercover courier in that area for Chang Kai-shek's espionage system.

For months everything went smoothly. Eva felt proud that she was helping in this small way. As an added bonus, the intelligence officer gave her information on the whereabouts of some of her family members who were still in Communist China.

One day while shopping, she was stopped by the Communist police. They had suspected Eva for some time and insisted on searching her. They took her to a police station where a woman searched her and all of her belongings. She found nothing and let Eva go. But Eva was carrying a message in a microdot as small as a pinpoint, placed on the inside of one of her hairpins. Once out of sight of the police, Eva delivered the microscopic message.

That evening when Eva stepped onto the stage, she hadn't expected to see the policemen. She knew that the Communists must still suspect her. Did they know her contact was at the show? If seen together, she and the other agent would be arrested. As the music to the purification dance began, it came to her. She knew how to warn her contact right under the noses of the Communist officers. She would simply add a new ending to the dance.

As the dance ended, Eva slowly kneeled and placed the brass bowl on the floor before her. She took the dagger from her sash and cut a long gash down the length of her arm. With a dramatic gesture, she ran the white chrysanthemum along the dripping wound, then held the blood-red flower above her head. She smiled. The audience was spellbound by the new ending.

Spy Trivia

A microdot is a photo negative the size of the period at the end of this sentence. With the help of a microscope, an agent can read every word on the microdot.

Eva's contact was not. He knew there was trouble. After the performance, he met her at a side door, and they slipped into the night. Eva never danced at the night-club again.

No one is sure where Eva and her contact went. Some say Eva traveled to Taiwan, where she joined some of her brothers. She may, or may not, be alive today. But whatever happened to Eva Wu, no one will ever forget the courage of this daring dancer.

The Cold War

After World War II ended, a new era in spying began. The Cold War started between the Soviet Union and the United States when the Soviet Union set up Communist governments in the countries of Eastern Europe liberated by their army during World War II. Germany was divided in two. The United States, France, and Britain controlled the western part of Germany, while the Soviet Union controlled the eastern part. Germany's capital city, Berlin, was divided into East and West, and the Berlin Wall was built by the Soviets so that people from the East couldn't escape to the West.

Communist spy networks were directed against many western countries. The United States responded by creating the CIA, the National Security Agency (NSA), and the Defense Intelligence Agency (DIA). These organizations gathered and analyzed foreign intelligence information. Berlin, Geneva, Vienna, and Mexico City became international centers of spying activity. In this era of mistrust, women found many opportunities to spy.

Tension between the United States and the Soviet Union eased in the late 1960s and again in the 1980s, when agreements to curb the arms race were signed. Reforms in the Soviet Union led to demands by other Communist countries for free elections. Communism collapsed in Eastern Europe, and the Berlin Wall was taken down. By 1990 the Cold War was over.

JONNA HIESTAND MENDEZ

Disguise Master

1945 –

Jonna worked her magic. The slight, clean-shaven man with the birth-mark on his face was gone. In his place stood an older, gray-haired, mustached fellow with glasses and a smooth complexion. But would the clever disguise be good enough?

Jonna Mendez was a CIA officer who specialized in disguises, fake docu-mentation, and clandestine photography. Intelligence officers like Jonna worked in the field providing spies with the methods and devices to do their work. On this assignment, Jonna was part of a plan to steal KAPELLE, a top-secret Soviet communication device. The high-profile operation was a big risk and could cause retaliation against American targets elsewhere in the world. Her disguise work would have to be her best yet.

* * * *

Jonna Hiestand was born in 1945 in Campbellsville, Kentucky, and grew up in Kansas. Both of her parents worked for Boeing Aircraft, her father as a mechanic and her mother in the computer sector. Jonna was one of four daughters.

As a girl Jonna was quiet but independent. She liked school and espe-cially enjoyed studying languages and foreign cultures. Being shy and quiet didn't stop her from getting into mischief—like pouring liquid soap into the town fountain. Jonna got a taste of travel early on when her family would pile into the car for cross-country trips to visit relatives.

Jonna also liked art, particularly painting and photography. She later explained, "Throughout my career, these interests seemed to guide me. I became a professional photographer, instructing foreign agents around the world. When I went into the field of disguise, it was my knowledge of art, colors, mediums, and composition that gave my work an original dimension. A good eye is important in the disguise field."[1]

In 1966, while living in Europe, Jonna met a young group of professionals who turned out to be CIA officers. Jonna found her new friends intriguing and decided to join the agency. At first she worked for the CIA overseas as a secretary, then continued in Washington, DC, rising up through the ranks to become a technical operations officer and finally, the CIA's Chief of Disguise.

The CIA sent Jonna on assignments overseas in 1987. Her area of operation covered territory from Pakistan to Burma, and from Sri Lanka to the Himalayas. Jonna was part of a unit that could do just about anything. Need to break into an office? Steal a code book? Photograph a document? No problem. What Jonna and her group could do wasn't far off from what happens in the James Bond movies. For the KAPELLE operation, Jonna was to provide the right type of cover for the team so their true identities would not become known.

Jonna and the team leader, "Cooper," drove to a hotel in the center of town where they rented a room with a view of their target: the Soviet compound. The room would serve as their observation post. One of Jonna's first jobs was to take photographs of the compound.

From "Cooper," she learned that this Soviet compound was short staffed. Many had gone on vacation, so the security wouldn't be as tight. She also learned that the KAPELLE device was inside one of the buildings in a specially secure room called the Sanctum.

The Sanctum was built like a bank vault with thick walls and a huge metal door. No key could open this door. It was locked with dead bolts and combination locks. Inside the Sanctum, the team would find the

KAPELLE bolted to the floor. Taking the KAPELLE would be a "smoking bolt operation" (CIA slang for describing the swiftness of a snatch, as in "There was nothing left but the smoking bolts on the floor."[2])

A local CIA agent, code name TUGBOAT, was to help them get into the building, but he needed a disguise, one that would give him a new look yet allow him to blend in on the street. TUGBOAT had already taken big risks working on other jobs for the CIA. People knew him in town. He'd need to be unrecognizable to help with the KAPELLE job. When they met, Jonna was distressed to see a large birthmark running down the right side of his face. How could she cover that up?

Jonna needed a lot of disguise materials to begin transforming TUG-BOAT. She got cosmetics from case officers' wives—foundation, powder, eye-liner, eyebrow pencil, anything. She also asked the staff to pool their disguise kits which were issued to each case officer before he or she left for an overseas assignment.

The next day Jonna met TUGBOAT in a safe house. She picked through the pile of cosmetics heaped on the dining room table—even a can of Dr. Scholl's foot powder might prove useful. She lined up applicators, towels, a brush, comb, and a mirror. Then she sat TUGBOAT down in a chair and got to work.

One hour later Jonna was done. Another intelligence officer who knew TUGBOAT hardly recognized him. TUGBOAT was ready.

In his new disguise, TUGBOAT approached the guard at the Soviet compound, showed him a fake police ID card (another one of Jonna's

Spy Trivia

Spy satellites orbiting the earth 250 miles away can make out objects as small as a grapefruit.

tricks), and explained that he was conducting a routine check of all the locks on the buildings. The guard hesitated but readily opened the gate when TUGBOAT handed him a roll of money. Once inside, TUGBOAT made careful measurements of the locks on the outer doors. He took them back to the snatch team who cut a key to fit each lock.

Spy Trivia

In Washington, DC you can visit the International Spy Museum or go online at: www.spymuseum.org

The team was just about ready to move. Jonna checked everyone's disguises and insisted that they practice their new identities, walking and driving around town until they felt comfortable in their covers.

On the night of the operation, the whole Soviet staff was away at a hunting camp. It was cool and the humidity had lessened, good for keeping the disguises intact. The last thing they needed were disguises melting off their faces! They traveled to the compound and stopped at the gate. The guard believed the disguised TUGBOAT was bringing in a team of security experts to do a surprise inspection of the compound. TUGBOAT gave the guard another roll of money, and the guard opened the gate and left. The van backed up to the central building and the snatch began.

It went like clockwork. The snatch team got through the outer doors with their new keys. The specially locked door inside gave them no problems either. Their training and expertise had given them the capability to penetrate any security system. They removed KAPELLE from the Soviet stronghold, slipped it into the van, and had it out of the country—all in less than twenty-four hours. Everyone's cover remained intact, thanks to Jonna's skill.

Jonna continued to work overseas on other assignments, developing her disguise magic. In one of her last operations, she teamed up with Tony Mendez, a previous Chief of Disguise for the CIA, to head a group of officers in a risky and complicated plan to help a Russian source escape Moscow. Later, she and Tony married.

Now they are both retired from the CIA and live in Maryland with their son, Jesse. Jonna, a professional photographer and author, teaches at an intelligence school and is on the Board of Directors for the International Spy Museum in Washington, DC. In addition, she and her husband consult for a CBS spy show called "The Agency," and speak to various groups in the intelligence community.

Of her career, Jonna says, "Young teens in today's somewhat overwhelming society might find it interesting to realize that one person can still make a difference in the world. A lot of my work gave me a steady sense of satisfaction that I think few jobs can provide. Some lives were protected, some threats overcome, and the United States benefited. I left the work feeling that it had been worthwhile. I made a contribution when it counted. What more can we hope for? I am so proud to have been part of the history of the Cold War and the years immediately after."[3]

SPY PROFILE:
Stella Rimington's Persistence

Dame Stella Rimington began her Secret Service career in 1965 in India. She had traveled there as the wife of a diplomat and got a part-time job with the local MI5 (the United Kingdom's Secret Service) representative. When she returned to London, she continued working for MI5 full time. Dame Stella soon realized that it was her dream career, but she knew it would be an uphill battle. She would have to fight the perception that women were not suited for certain roles, like meeting human intelligence sources (people who might be terrorists). But Dame Stella persisted, even when she became a single parent.

She worked her way up through the ranks for twenty-two years and in 1991 was named the director general. She was MI5's first female head. Dame Stella oversaw key departments like counterterrorism, counter espionage, and countersubversion. She strove for a policy of greater openness, believing that the public should know more about the Service and the extent of its responsibilities. She was the first leader whose name was made public during her term.

NOTES

Josephine Baker

1. Josephine Baker, as quoted by Ean Wood, *The Josephine Baker Story* (London: Sanctuary Publishing Ltd, 2000), p. 222.

2. Ibid. p. 214.

3. Ibid. p. 301.

Mary Bowser

1. Military Intelligence, Apr-Jun 1995, as quoted by Susan Robinson, "Mary Elizabeth Bowser," *A Day in Black History, 8/27/01* (www.gibbsmagazine.com).

Belle Boyd

1. Curtis C. Davis, ed., *Belle Boyd in Camp and Prison, Written by Herself* (New York: Thomas Yoseleff, 1968), p. 167.

Pauline Cushman

1. As quoted by F.L. Sarmiento, *Life of Pauline Cushman* (Philadelphia: John E. Potter & Co., 1865), p. 62.

2. Ibid. p. 67.

3. New York Times, May 28, 1864, as quoted by Elizabeth D. Leonard, *All the Daring of the Soldier* (New York: W.W. Norton & Co., 1999), p. 58.

Lydia Darragh

1. Elizabeth D. Leonard, *All the Daring of the Soldier* (New York: W.W. Norton & Co., 1999), p. 25.

Josefa Ortiz de Dominguez

1. Josefa Ortiz, as quoted by Jerome R. Adams, *Notable Latin American*

Women: Twenty-nine Leaders, Rebels, Poets, Battlers and Spies, 1500–1900 (Jefferson, N.C.: McFarland & Co., 1995), p. 88.

Virginia Hall

1. Pierre Fayol, *Chambon-sur-Lignon sous l'occupation*, as quoted by Elizabeth P. McIntosh, *Sisterhood of Spies* (New York: Dell Publishing, 1998), p. 335.

2. V. Hall and London official as quoted by Pierre Fayol. *Le Chambon-sur-Lignon sous l'occupation (1940–1944).* (Paris: Edition L'Hartmattan, 1990), 118.

3. V. Hall, as quoted by Gerald K. Haines, "Virginia Hall Goillot, Career Intelligence Officer," *Prologue Quarterly of the National Archives*, 26, 4 (Winter 1991): p. 249–260. (www.cia.gov/cia/ciakids/history)

Noor Inayat Khan

1. Jean Overton Fuller, *Madeleine: The Story of Noor Inayat Khan* (London: Victor Gollancz Ltd., 1952), p. 38.

2. Noor Inayat Khan, *Twenty Jataka Tales* (Rochester, Vt.: Inner Traditions International, 1975, East-West Publications, Ltd., 1985), p. 51.

Gertrude Legendre

1.Gertrude S. Legendre, *The Time of My Life.* (Charleston, S.C.: Wyrick and Company, 1987), p. 173.

2. Ibid, p.173.

Elizabeth Van Lew

1. William Gilmore Beymer, "Miss Van Lew," *Harpers Monthly*, June 1911 (www.mdgorman.com/Miss%20Van%20Lew.htm).

2. Elizabeth Van Lew, *A Yankee Spy in Richmond, The Civil War Diary of "Crazy Bet" Van Lew*, ed. David D. Ryan (Mechanicsburg, Pa.: Stackpole Books, 1996), p.22.

Maria Gulovich Liu

1. NARA RG 226 Entry 108B84F691 Box 84 Folder 691, as quoted by Elizabeth P. McIntosh, *Sisterhood of Spies* (New York: Dell Publishing, 1998), 198.

Jonna Hiestand Mendez

1. Jonna Mendez, Personal Communication.
2. Jonna Mendez, *Spy Dust* (New York: ATRIA Books, 2002), 63.
3. Jonna Mendez, Personal Communication.

Leona Vicario Roo

1. Jerome R. Adams, *Notable Latin American Women: Twenty-nine Leaders, Rebels, Poets, Battlers and Spies, 1500–1900* (Jefferson, N.C.: McFarland & Co., 1995), p. 118.

Policarpa Salaverrieta

1. Policarpa Salavarrieta, as quoted by James D. Henderson and Linda Roddy Henderson, *Ten Notable Women of Latin America* (Chicago: Nelson-Hall, Inc., 1978), p. 119.

Laodicea Langston Springfield

1. Greenville (SC) Mountaineer, June 10, 1837, as quoted by EZ Langston, "Laodicea Langston: 'Daring Dicey'" (www.geocities.com/Heartland/Estates/ 2932/ dicey.html).

Harriet Tubman

1. Harriet Tubman, as quoted by M.W. Taylor, *Harriet Tubman, Antislavery Activist* (Philadelphia: Chelsea House Publishers, 1991), p.37.
2. William Still, as quoted by Nancy A. Davidson, "Harriet Tubman, 'Moses,'" *Notable Black American Women*, ed. Jessie Carney Smith (Detroit: Gale Research, 1992), p. 1153.

Patience Lovell Wright

1. George Washington, as quoted by Charles Coleman Sellers, *Patience Wright: American Artist and Spy in George III's London* (Middletown, Conn.: Wesleyan University Press, 1976), p. 193.

RESOURCES

The Anglo-Dutch Wars

Aphra Behn

Blashfield, Evangeline W. *Portraits and Backgrounds.* New York: Charles Schribenrs Sons, 1917.

Goreau, Angeline. *Reconstructing Aphra: A Social Biography of Aphra Behn.* New York: Dial Press, 1980.

Todd, Janet M. *The Secret Life of Aphra Behn.* Piscataway, N.J.: Rutgers University Press, 1997.

The American Revolution

Lydia Darragh

Drinker, Sophie H. "Lydia Barrington Darragh," *Notable American Women, 1607-1950: A Biographical Dictionary*, eds. Edward T. James and Janet W. James. Cambridge, Mass.: The Belknap Press of Harvard University Press, 1971.

Hoehling, A.A. *Women Who Spied.* New York: Dodd, Mead & Co., 1967.

Leonard, Elizabeth D. *All the Daring of the Soldier.* New York: W.W. Norton & Co., 1999.

Zeinert, Karen. *Those Remarkable Women of the American Revolution.* Brookfield, Conn.: The Millford Press, 1996.

Emily Geiger

Clark, Frank O., Webmaster. *Emily Geiger, A Set of Source Documents.* Published online at www.sciway3.net/clark/revolutionarywar/ geigeroutline.html

Ellet, Elizabeth F. *Women of the American Revolution. vol. 2.* New York: Baker and Scribner, 1850.

Imrey, Harriet. Personal Communication.

Anna Smith Strong

Currie, Catherine. *Anna Smith Strong and the Setauket Spy Ring.* Port Jefferson, N.Y.: Precise Printing, Inc., 1992.

"Spy Letters of the American Revolution." Collections of the Clements Library. Published online at www.si.umich.edu/spies

Tylor, Beverly C. "The Setauket Spies." E. Setauket, N.Y.: Three Village Historical Society, 2001. Published online at members.aol.com/ TVHS1/18thcent.html

Patience Lovell Wright

Sellers, Charles Coleman. *Patience Wright: American Artist and Spy in George III's London.* Middletown, Conn.: Wesleyan University Press, 1976.

Laodicea Langston Springfield

Ellet, Elizabeth F. *Women of the American Revolution. vol. 1.* New York: Baker and Scribner, 1850.

Langston, E.Z. "Laodicea Langston: 'Daring Dicey.'" Published online at www.geocities.com/Heartland/Estates/2932/dicey.html

The Wars of Independence in Spanish America

Josefa Ortiz de Dominguez

Adams, Jerome R. *Notable Latin American Women: Twenty-nine Leaders, Rebels, Poets, Battlers and Spies, 1500-1900*. Jefferson, N.C.: McFarland & Co., 1995.

Anzures, Rafael. *Colección de biografías de los principales héroes de la independencia*. Tlaxcala: Oficina Tipográfica del Gobierno, 1909.

Gugliotta, Bobette. *Women of Mexico: The Consecrated and the Commoners, 1519-1900*. Encino, Calif.: Floricanto Press, 1989.

Sosa, Francisco. *Biografías de Mexicanos distinguidos*. Mexico, D.F.: Editorial Porrúa, 1884.

Leona Vicario Roo

Adams, Jerome R. *Notable Latin American Women: Twenty-nine Leaders, Rebels, Poets, Battlers and Spies, 1500-1900*. Jefferson, NC: McFarland & Co., 1995.

Anzures, Rafael. *Colección de biografías de los principales héroes de la independencia*. Tlaxcala: Oficina Tipográfica del Gobierno, 1909.

Gugliotta, Bobette. *Women of Mexico: The Consecrated and the Commoners, 1519-1900*. Encino, Calif.: Floricanto Press, 1989.

Sosa, Francisco. *Biografías de Mexicanos distinguidos*. Mexico, D.F.: Editorial Porrúa, 1884.

Policarpa Salaverrieta

Adams, Jerome R. *Notable Latin American Women: Twenty-nine Leaders, Rebels, Poets, Battlers and Spies, 1500-1900*. Jefferson, N.C.: McFarland & Co., 1995.

DuBois, Jill and Leslie Jermyn. *Colombia*. Tarrytown, N.Y.: Benchmark Books, 2002.

Henderson, James D. and Linda Roddy Henderson. *Ten Notable Women of Latin America*. Chicago: Nelson-Hall, Inc., 1978.

The Civil War

Harriet Tubman

Bradford, Sarah. *Harriet Tubman: The Moses of Her People*. Gloucester, Mass.: Peter Smith, 1981.

Davidson, Nancy A. "Harriet Tubman: 'Moses.'" *Notable Black American Women*. Jessie Carney Smith, ed. Detroit: Gale Research, 1992.

Taylor, M.W. *Harriet Tubman, Antislavery Activist*. Philadelphia: Chelsea House Publishers, 1991.

Freedom Quilts

Tobin, Jacqueline L. and Raymond G. Dobard, Ph.D. *Hidden in Plain View: A Secret Story of Quilts and the Underground Railroad*. New York: Doubleday, 1999.

Wilson, Sule Greg C. *African American Quilting: The Warmth of Tradition*. New York: The Rosen Publishing Group, Inc., 1999.

Elizabeth Van Lew

Beymer, William Gilmore. "Miss Van Lew." *Harpers Monthly*, June 1911. Published online at www.mdgorman.com/Miss%20Van %20Lew.htm

Van Lew, Elizabeth. *A Yankee Spy in Richmond: The Civil War Diary of*

"Crazy Bet" Van Lew. David D. Ryan, ed. Mechanicsburg, Pa.: Stackpole Books, 1996.

Zeinert, Karen. *Elizabeth Van Lew: Southern Belle, Union Spy*. Parsippany, N.J.: Dillon Press, 1995.

Mary Bowser

Jones, Katharine M. *Ladies of Richmond*. Indianapolis: The Bobbs-Merrill Co., Inc., 1962.

Peterson, Harriette A. "Mary Elizabeth Bowser." *Notable Black American Women*. Jessie Carney Smith, ed. Detroit: Gale Research, 1992.

Robinson, Susan. "Mary Elizabeth Bowser." *A Day in Black History*, 8/27/01. Published online at www.gibbsmagazine.com

Belle Boyd

Leonard, Elizabeth D. *All the Daring of the Soldier*. New York: W.W. Norton & Co., 1999.

Martini, Teri. *The Secret is Out—True Spy Stories*. Boston: Little Brown, 1990.

Davis, Curtis, C., ed. *Belle Boyd in Camp and Prison, Written By Herself*. New York: Thomas Yoseloff, 1968.

Pauline Cushman

Kane, Harnett T. *Spies for the Blue and Gray*. Garden City, New York: Hanover House, 1954.

Leonard, Elizabeth D. *All the Daring of the Soldier*. New York: W.W. Norton & Co., 1999.

Sarmiento, F.L. *Life of Pauline Cushman*. Philadelphia: John E. Potter & Co., 1865.

Sarah Emma Edmonds

Dannett, Sylvia G.L. *She Rode with the Generals*. New York: Thomas Nelson & Sons, 1960.

Hall, Richard. *Patriots in Disguise: Women Warriors of the Civil War*. New York: Marlowe & Co., 1993.

Leonard, Elizabeth D. *All the Daring of the Soldier*. New York: W.W. Norton & Co., 1999.

Steven, Bryna. *Frank Thompson, Her Civil War Story*. New York: Macmillan Publishers Co., 1992.

World War I

Louise de Bettignies

Hoeling, A.A. *Women Who Spied*. New York: Dodd, Mead & Co., 1967.

Mahoney, M.H. *Women In Espionage, A Biographical Dictionary*. Santa Barbara, Calif.: ABC-CLIO, 1993.

Seth, Ronald. *Some of My Favorite Spies*. Philadelphia: Chilton Book Co., 1968.

Marthe Richer

Franklin, Charles. *The Great Spies*. New York: Hart Publishing, 1988.

Mahoney, M. H. *Women in Espionage, A Biographical Dictionary*. Santa Barbara, Calif.: ABC-CLIO, 1993.

The Penguin Biographical Dictionary of Women, Market Books Ltd., 1998. Published online at www.xrefer.com/entry/173242

Mata Hari
Howe, Russell Warren. *Mata Hari, The True Story*. New York: Dodd, Mead & Co., 1986.

Marguerite Harrison
Mahoney, M.H. *Women in Espionage: A Biographical Dictionary*. Santa Barbara, Calif.: ABC-CLIO, 1993.

Olds, Elizabeth F. *Women of the Four Winds*. Boston: Houghton Mifflin Company, 1985.

World War II
Virginia Hall
Casey, Dennis. "Limping Lady Begins Spy Career in Early 1940s." Published online at www.64-baker-street.org/html

McIntosh, Elizabeth P. *Sisterhood of Spies*. New York: Dell Publishing, 1998.

Rossiter, Margaret L. *Women in the Resistance*. New York: Praeger, 1986

Josephine Baker
Papich, Stephen. *Remembering Josephine*. Indianapolis/New York: The Bobbs Merrill Co., Inc., 1976.

Wood, Ean. *The Josephine Baker Story*. London: Sanctuary Publishing Ltd, 2000.

Noor Inayat Khan

Fuller, Jean Overton. *Madeleine: The Story of Noor Inayat Khan*. London: Victor Gollancz, Ltd., 1952.

Khan, Noor Inayat. *Twenty Jataka Tales*. Rochester, Vt.: Inner Traditions International, 1975, 1985, East-West Publications, Ltd.

Gertrude S. Legendre

Legendre, Gertrude, S. *The Time of My Life*. Charleston, S.C.: Wyrick and Company, 1987.

Idem. The Sands Ceased to Run. New York: William Frederick Press, 1947.

Betty Pack

Lovell, Mary S. *Cast No Shadow, the Life of the American Spy Who Changed the Course of World War II*. New York: Pantheon Books, 1992.

McIntosh, Elizabeth P. *Sisterhood of Spies*. New York: Dell Publishing, 1998.

Sullivan, George. *In the Line of Fire: Eight Women War Spies*. New York: Scholastic, 1996.

Maria Gulovich Liu

Downs, Jim. *World War II: OSS Tragedy in Slovakia*. Oceanside, Calif.; Liefrinck Publishers, 2002.

Liu, Maria Gulovich. Oxnard, Calif., December 10, 2002.

McIntosh, Elizabeth P. *Sisterhood of Spies*. New York: Dell Publishing, 1998.

The Chinese Revolution

Eva Wu

Mahoney, M.H. *Women in Espionage: A Biographical Dictionary.* Santa
    Barbara, Calif.: ABC-CLIO, 1993.

Singer, Kurt. *Spy Stories from Asia.* New York: Wilfred Funk, Inc., 1955.

The Cold War

Jonna Hiestand Mendez

Mendez, Antonio and Jonna Mendez. *Spy Dust.* New York: ATRIA Books,
2002.

Mendez, Jonna. Personal Communication.

Spy Facts

Platt, Richard. *Eyewitness Spy: Discover the World of Espionage.* New York:
    DK Publishing, 2000.

Owen, David. *Hidden Secrets: A Complete History of Espionage and the
    Technology Used to Support It.* Toronto: Firefly Books, 2002.

ML   11/04